MUSINGS ON ISSUES IN THE NEWS

PETER OVIE AKUS

DEDICATION

I dedicate this book to my Creator who blessed me with the gift of
writing

CONTENTS

ACKNOWLEDGMENTS

I am profoundly grateful and eternally indebted to everyone who has played one role or the other in making this book a reality

MUSINGS ON ISSUES IN THE NEWS

PREAMBLE

This book is a collection of essays about my thoughts on critical issues that pertain to the Nigerian State. It is a melting pot of *letters*, *articles*, *commentaries*, and *blog posts* which have been published on various media platforms over the years. While some of the events written in this book may have been overtaken by other events, thus seeming irrelevant to today, the complexities of the Nigerian State is such that the same issues keep revolving over and over again, which makes the panaceas proffered in this book relevant today.

MUSINGS ON ISSUES IN THE NEWS

MUSINGS ON ISSUES IN THE NEWS

MR. PRESIDENT, PLEASE STOP THIS BLOODSHED

I write in reaction to President Goodluck Jonathan's statement on New Year day that all the Boko Haram suspects responsible for the various attacks in the country have been apprehended. The President also gave himself kudos for preventing a wave of terror attacks from the extremist sect during the Yuletide. I beg to say that this is nothing but unnecessary vain-glorying.

All over the world, leaders are always privy to information that the general populace does not possess. This is why they are people of few words; this is so that they do not reveal sensitive information which are inimical to their interests. An example is President Obama having knowledge of Osama bin Laden's whereabouts a year before the operation to take him out was eventually carried out.

President Jonathan in all honesty cannot say he does not know those behind these attacks. Then why do we have the SSS, DMI, DDI, Police, Army, Navy, Air-Force, NIA, e.t.c? All these agencies submit daily reports to the President yet he is in a quandary about what to do. I know that he might not have enough evidence to arrest these evil fellows but he can employ Machiavellian principles to bully these fellows to stop their fiendish acts.

This will also create an image of strength thereby helping his Presidency. Let us not forget that Former President Obasanjo employed these tactics between 2003 to 2007 to pursue his objectives. No wonder Baba as he is fondly called cried out recently that Jonathan is doing nothing while Nigeria gradually slides into the abyss.

Great heroes are birthed from the womb of great crises. Let him put aside political considerations, because if he fails to act now, he will forever be consigned to the dustbin of history and posterity will never forgive him.

January 9, 2013.

THE MILITARY AND THEIR LEGACIES

As we celebrate our fallen heroes this week, one area often neglected by most Nigerians is the contributions of our military towards the development of our nation. This is because military rule has always been associated with evils like corruption, nepotism, and other evils. But we also forget that they contributed a great deal to some of the progress that we have experienced as a nation in the last 52 years.

The most important contribution of the military to our nation is keeping us united as one country. The military fought a 30-month civil war which consumed several of its brightest minds like Major Kaduna Nzeogwu, Emmanuel Ifeajuna and Colonel Victor Banjo to mention a few. If the politicians were the ones that were in power at that time, I am sure that they would have conducted referendum in the various regions and there would be no Nigeria today.

Most of the infrastructures we have in our country today were built by the military. The military also built several roads and bridges which dot the nook and cranny of the state. Let us not forget that Abuja as a city was built by the military. They also built several airports and seaports that we have in our country today.

In the education sector, the military built several Unity Schools in various states of the federation. They also built several universities thereby enhancing the availability of manpower to aid us in our drive towards industrial and technological greatness.

Most of the power stations through which electricity is provided to most Nigerians were built by the military. In fact, the regime of General Muhammadu Buhari almost solved the problem of erratic power supply in our country before it was overthrown. The failure of successive administrations to make critical investments in that sector has left us where we are today.

All our refineries were built by the military and they were in good working condition. Since 1999 till now our politicians have not succeeded in building a single refinery instead they increase the pump price of fuel every year and yet there is a disparity in prices among the various states of the federation.

Nigeria experienced her greatest sporting glory under military rule. The Super Eagles won the African Cup of Nations in 1994, Gold in Men's Football in Atlanta 1996; the Golden Eaglets won the U-17 World Cup in 1985, Nigeria's first Gold Medalist, Chioma Ajunwa (1996) among many other sporting victories.

I am not advocating a return to military rule but it is high time our politicians stop blaming the military for our woes 14 years into our democratic voyage. Let them instead concentrate on how to take us to the promised land.

January 15, 2013.

MISSING-IN-ACTION GOVERNORS

Many years ago, I read a work of fiction about a governor in Nigeria who was kidnapped. There was confusion everywhere and the Head of State ordered that he must be found either dead or alive. The book has become somehow prophetic because how can one explain the sudden disappearance of the governors of Enugu, Taraba and Cross River states? The only difference is that there seems to be quietness in high places giving a semblance that all is well.

Nobody has seen or heard from the Enugu State Governor Sullivan Chime for close to six months. He wrote a letter to the House of Assembly intimating them of his intention to go on accumulated leave for three months and mandated his deputy Sunday Onyebuchi to act on his behalf. Now six months down the line we have not heard or seen him with rumours that he is in India or as some say, London. The ship of state is gradually grinding to a halt with the acting governor afraid to carry out his responsibilities while the Chief of Staff is running the show behind the scenes. This is reminiscent of the Yar'adua era. The ghost of Yar'adua lives on.

Taraba State Governor Danbaba Suntai was involved in a plane crash with his private jet near Yola, Adamawa State. He has since been flown to Germany for medical treatment but since then nothing has been heard from him. Two photos of him were released recently but instead of quelling rumours that he is brain dead and might be an invalid for life, they seem to reinforce it. In those pictures, he is expressionless and seems not to recognise those he took the pictures with. They include his wife and children as well as his fellow governor Jonah Jang of Plateau State. His deputy, who is now the Acting Governor, has since taken charge but he is also afraid of carrying out his responsibilities. In fact, on the day of the crash, a certain Senator in the state mobilized thugs to chase him from the government house to prevent him from becoming governor.

In Cross River State, the governor has also been gone for a long time allegedly for medical treatment. Nobody has seen or heard from him and the statement by the Senate Leader Victor Ndoma Egba that he was with him in the US and that he is hale and hearty looks more like a political talk.

Many people have commended the Kogi State Governor Idris Wada for seeking medical treatment in Nigeria instead of abroad after he was involved in a fatal car crash. But he did that to preserve his office not because of patriotism. The fear of his enemies is the beginning of wisdom.

The only reason our political office holders prefer to die in office is because of filthy lucre. Even when they are sick and want to hand-over or tell Nigerians their true medical state, they often face opposition from political aides, associates and hangers on whose source of livelihood depends on the political office holder whether legitimately or not.

My advice to deputy governors in Enugu, Taraba and Cross River is that they should be patriotic and rule courageously irrespective of whose ox is gored. After all, their principals are second term governors. They therefore have nothing to lose.

January 21, 2013.

POLICE COLLEGE IKEJA: MATTERS ARISING

I watched with shock and disbelief the Channels Television documentary on the Nigerian Police College, Ikeja. That place is an eyesore. That this is Nigeria's premier police training college beats my imagination. How did such an institution which has produced several great police officers, including a former President of Botswana fall into such a sorry state of disrepair?

We need a total overhaul of the police in order to position it to meet the security challenges in our country. We need to examine staff welfare. How much are our policemen paid? Do they have adequate insurance for their lives if killed in the line of duty? Are their pensions and gratuity paid as at when due? What about their housing conditions?

A situation in which policemen pay for their own uniforms and boots does not speak well of us as a nation. When Nigerian policemen are sent on peace-keeping missions outside the shores of our land, they perform very well. They even win medals for their efforts. But these are the same policemen who are unable to perform here.

Training is very essential if we want our policemen to perform their duties optimally. The current state of disrepair of the police college is very shameful. How can men who are trained under such circumstances turn out to be agents of change in the society? Can you imagine the psychological torture they go through?

They can only graduate to take revenge on the society. Let our police colleges spread across the length and breadth of this country be renovated and refurbished to meet modern standards. Our policemen should also be sent on crash courses outside the country, so that they can see how policing is done in modern societies. They should be trained in the use of ICT as we now live in a digital age. Their weaponry should be upgraded.

President Jonathan's statement that someone was out to embarrass the government is nothing but playing to the gallery. He should bring to book those responsible for the state of disrepair in the Police College. Mr. John Momoh, chairman of Channels Television is a patriot and should be commended for his work of investigative journalism.

January 25, 2013.

GANI ADAMS AND AARE ONA KAKANFO

Though I am not Yoruba, I feel constrained to comment on the appointment of Chief Gani Adams as the 15th Aare Ona Kakanfo of Yorubaland. For the benefit of non-Yorubas like me who may not understand what and who the Aare Ona Kakanfo is, permit me to elucidate a bit.

In the Ancient Oyo Empire, they operated a form of federal structure long before the coming of the Europeans. The head was the Alaafin who was supported by the Oyomesi which was the ruling council headed by the Bashorun who is the Prime Minister. They also had the Eshos who were responsible for maintaining law and order in the society.

The Ogboni Society acted as judges who not only settled disputes but were responsible for ensuring that the customs and traditions of the land were upheld. The Aare Ona Kakanfo was the Generalissimo. He was the Commander-in-Chief of the Armed Forces. He lived outside the capital city and anytime he entered the capital, the Alaafin had to abdicate his position as that is tantamount to a coup d'etat. Furthermore, he was expected to be a brave and fearless warrior who must never suffer defeat in battle else he must voluntarily commit suicide.

In today's 21st century, where we no longer have kingdoms but countries, republics and states, the AAre Ona Kakanfo is largely a symbolic and ceremonial office. That does not however, diminish the importance of the title as it is expected that the holder must be someone who is cerebral, charismatic, courageous and selfless as he is representing one of the most advanced races in the world whose tentacles spread as far as Brazil and Cuba. The last two holders of the title Chief Ladoke Akintola, Former Premier of the Western Region and Chief M.K.O Abiola, businessman, philanthropist and the presumed winner of the June 12, 1993 Presidential elections were titans who despite their flaws, gave their all to their people.

The appointment of Chief Gani Adams as the 15th Aare Ona Kakanfo has left a sour taste in the mouth of many Yorubas. This is because he largely epitomizes everything that is the antithesis of what is expected of the holder of that office. As the leader of the Oodua Peoples' Congress (OPC), he unleashed a reign of terror on his people killing, maiming, and carrying out extra-judicial killings which prompted the Former President Chief Olusegun Obasanjo to proscribe the group in the year 2000. Obasanjo also went ahead to label the group as a terrorist organization and gave the security agencies a mandate to shoot-at-sight any OPC member they found.

This same Gani Adams was charged to court for treason in 2007. In the last general elections in 2015, he openly supported the Peoples' Democratic Party and Former President Goodluck Jonathan. He paraded his members on Ikorodu road in Lagos wielding dangerous weapons like guns, sticks, knives, charms, amulets and dressed in hoods and balaclavas in order to intimidate Lagosians not to support the All Progresssive Congress (APC). But he failed woefully. The Yorubas have now become a laughing stock in the eyes of other tribes and ethnic groups in Nigeria because they have given a revered position meant for enigmatic and larger than life personalities to a Lilliputian. However, all hope is not lost as the recent reversal of the goodwill ambassadorial appointment given to Zimbabwean President Robert Mugabe by the World Health Organization (W.H.O) has shown that there is indeed no decision that is irreversible in this world.

October 26, 2017.

KACHIKWU VERSUS BARU

Since the news broke last week of the memo to the President, written by the Minister of State for Petroleum Resources, Dr. Emmanuel Ibe Kachikwu on August 30th 2017, raising sundry allegations against the Group Managing Director of the Nigerian National Petroleum Corporation (NNPC), Dr. Maikanti Baru; It has been a series of allegations and counter-allegations from the camp of both men with many Nigerians taking sides with one camp or the other. It is important that we understand what the issues are and what they are not before we pass judgment or support one camp or the other.

Dr. Kachikwu raised three main issues in his memo. One, is that the GMD of NNPC unilaterally awarded contracts to the tune of $25 billion US Dollars without consulting the Board of NNPC. Two, that he ran a "bravado management" sidelining the Minister and the board. Three, is that he made appointments without consultation with the Minister or the Board. Nowhere in the memo did the Minister accuse Baru of corruption or allege that monies where missing as was the case during the Jonathan administration when the then Central Bank Governor and now Emir of Kano, Sanusi Lamido Sanusi alleged that about $49 billion US Dollars realized from crude oil sales was not remitted into the Federation Account by the NNPC.

That allegation by Sanusi was later proven to be true first by an International Audit firm engaged by the government of the day, and second by the corruption cases against Diezani Allison-Maduekwe, the

Former Minister of Petroleum, Jide Omokore and Kola Aluko who are both Oil Moguls. Now having established that indeed no money is missing or was stolen, the GMD of NNPC went ahead to clarify the issue of the contracts. According to him, there was no release of money to the International Oil Companies that won the contracts as the IOC's would source for the funds themselves and the share of the profits realized that pertains to the Federal Government would be paid directly into the Federation Account.

The real substance in all the allegations of Dr. Kachikwu against Dr. Baru is that, due process was not followed by the GMD and also his alleged insubordination to the Minister. The GMD has defended himself by saying he acted in line with the NNPC Act, the NNPC Handbook and the Public Procurement of 2007, which vests the power to award contracts and make critical appointments in the NNPC with the NNPC Tenders Board of which the GMD is Chairman, the Minister of Petroleum Resources which happens to be the President and the Federal Executive Council.

However, we must also not fail to note that there are gaps in the NNPC Act which stakeholders in the oil industry have argued would only be solved with the passage of the Petroleum Industry Bill. One of the many gaps is that, there is no mention of the Minister of State for Petroleum in the Act. That means that Kachikwu has now become like a *"spare tyre"* who will only work when the President wants him to work, as the President is the substantive Minister of Petroleum and Baru claimed he got all approvals from him which he (the President) is yet to refute.

Both Kachikwu and Baru are experienced technocrats who know their jobs and have made meaningful impact in the Petroleum Industry. Kachikwu as the GMD of NNPC helped resolve the problem of Joint Venture Cash Calls. He has also helped to influence the extension of exemption of Nigeria from the production cap by the Organization of Petroleum Exporting Countries. Baru on the other hand was the Former Chairman of the NNPC Anti-Corruption Committee. He has also helped to not only ensure unhindered petroleum product supply for all Nigerians but has also commenced exploration efforts in the

Frontier Basins especially those in the North, the most recent being the Sokoto Basin.

The President should call Kachikwu and Baru and resolve the matter amicably. He should establish a chain of command taking cognizance of Kachikwu's office and delegate some of his powers to Kachikwu. The National Assembly should also expedite action on the passage of the PIB bill so as to avoid crisis of this nature in the future.

October 27, 2017.

AN APPEAL TO GOVERNORS

In response to a news headline in the Nation Newspaper of Saturday 21st October, 2017 titled *"FG set to disburse fresh Paris Club refund"*. Ordinarily, this news should gladden the hearts of millions of Nigeria's public sector workers, but that is not the case. This is because about 23 states in Nigeria are currently indebted to workers. These workers include civil servants, local government workers, pensioners and even contractors.

Some of these state governments owe as much as a year salary arrears thereby causing untold hardship and pain to the families and dependents of these workers. The recent suicide of a Director in the Kogi State civil service due to financial hardship occasioned by the non-payment of salaries by the state government for 11 months speaks volumes of the misery and squalor that Nigerian workers currently wallow in due to inability of state governments to pay salaries and allowances of workers when it is due.

However, the problem did not begin today neither did it begin at the inception of the Muhammadu Buhari administration. It began in 2014 when global oil prices plummeted from $140 dollars a barrel to less than $50 dollars a barrel thereby triggering huge revenue shortages for Nigeria since we largely run a mono economy dependent on oil. The $40 billion dollars left in the Excess Crude Account by former President Olusegun Obasanjo in 2007 which was savings from the excess money realized from crude oil sales due to exceedingly high crude oil prices, had been depleted to zero.

The money in the Excess Crude Account was shared among the 36 state governors by the Yar'adua and Jonathan administrations due to pressure from the governors who said they needed the money for infrastructural development in their states and therefore saw no wisdom in saving money for tomorrow. It was meant to be savings for a rainy day but now that the rains have started falling, it is the ordinary Nigerian worker that is suffering from the effects of the rain.

Since President Muhammadu Buhari came on board in 2015, he has given out two bailout funds and two tranches of Paris Club refund to the state governments to enable them meet their obligations to workers, yet it seems the monies were diverted for other purposes other than that for which it was originally meant for since the narrative as regards the plight of workers is yet to change. Now that the federal government is about to release the third tranche of the Paris Club refund, I am appealing to the Governors to use the money to pay the workers' salaries, allowances and entitlements.

It goes against the grain for them to say that they cannot spend all the money paying workers' salaries alone while they continue to pay huge salaries and allowances to political office holders. The argument by some of them that civil servants constitute only 10% percent of the population of the state and so cannot consume 90% per cent of the resources is also not tenable as it is against the law of natural justice for a man to work for someone and not get rewarded after a period of time. Come to think of it, if they (governors) do not pay the workers who then do they expect to pay them seeing that they are employees of the state?

What the governors should do is to reduce their monthly wage bill by weeding out ghost workers. This can be easily done with the Bank Verification Number and the use of e-payment platforms to pay salaries. They should also cut down on their profligate lifestyle. Some of the governors who are owing salaries still own private jets. Others are erecting multi-million dollar statues while some of them still spend a whole week celebrating their birthdays. Let them also begin to think of ingenious ways of increasing the Internally Generated Revenue of their states. Asiwaju Bola Ahmed Tinubu did it during his tenure as Lagos State Governor when he was almost strangulated economically by the refusal of the then President Chief Olusegun Obasanjo to release funds meant for local governments in Lagos State. The era of dependence by the states on the federal government typified by the monthly odyssey to Abuja in order to suck from the federal breast is outdated and antiquated.

October 28, 2017.

OKOROCHA'S MISPLACED PRIORITIES

The erection of a statue by the Imo State governor, Owelle Anayo Rochas Okorocha in honour of the South African President Jacob Zuma has attracted criticism and condemnation from all quarters. Ordinarily, there is nothing wrong in building a statue to honour an accomplished and deserving individual but the personality involved is what is making many tongues wag.

Jacob Zuma does not deserve to be honoured in any way whatsoever by Okorocha. This is a man that is generally perceived to be corrupt by his people because of the numerous corruption cases that he has faced and is still facing. He is also seen as an immoral person due to the rape case that he faced some years ago and the defense which he gave. The fact that there have been seven attempts by the South African parliament to get him out of office is further proof of the fact that he is loathed by many in South Africa.

Governor Okorocha not only erected a statue in his honour, he also directed a traditional ruler in the state to give him a chieftaincy title. He awarded him the Imo Merit Award, named a road after him in Owerri and held a lavish banquet in his honour. All these were done with taxpayers' money, yet the governor owe workers' salaries and pensioners for as many as seven months.

He ordered the destruction of a popular traditional market in Owerri which led to the destruction of several properties and the loss of three lives a few months ago. Governor Okorocha owes contractors in the state to the tune of several billions of naira which he has been unable to pay till date. He spent hundreds of millions of naira constructing billboards all over the state depicting him shaking hands with the then US President Barack Obama some years ago. The fact that many Igbos have been killed in xenophobic attacks in South Africa most of them Imo State indigenes does not seem to bother Okorocha. Rather, he seems fascinated by Zuma's love for education. Yet, news reports emanating from South Africa indicate that there have been protests by students in South Africa in recent times owing to the government's poor funding of education.

Many Nigerian leaders from Murtala Muhammed to Ibrahim Babangida, private individuals like Chief M.K.O Abiola and musicians like the late Evangelist Sunny Okosun contributed money, sweat and blood to make South Africa free from apartheid. Yet, there is no monument erected in their honour in a free South Africa today, 23 years after the death of apartheid. What Okorocha has done is akin to a governor in America unveiling a statue in honour of the Nazi leader Adolf Hitler. That is impossibility and should it happen would only sound the death knell on the career of such a politician. But in Nigeria, all things are possible.

October 28, 2017.

RETURN OF JUSTICE SALAMI

The announcement by the National Judicial Council headed by the Chief Justice of Nigeria, Justice Walter Nkanu Onnoghen of the setting up of the Corruption and Financial Crimes Cases Trial Monitoring Committee has elicited a lot of positive reactions from Nigerians. This is because of the character that was selected to head the committee.

He is none other than Justice Ayo Salami, the former President of the Court of Appeal who exited the office six years ago in controversial circumstances. Justice Ayo Salami is reputed to be forthright and principled individual. One who is not afraid to speak truth to power irrespective of whose ox is gored. His antecedents as a jurist indeed speak volumes of his strength of character and also of his role as an impartial arbiter in the temple of justice.

The terms of reference of the committee are also another issue which has gladdened the hearts of millions of Nigerians. Two of the items stand out for mention here. One is to monitor courts handling of corruption cases and the second is to see to the creation of special courts in each judicial division in the country to handle corruption cases.

What this seeks to achieve is the speedy trial of corruption cases in Nigeria and the monitoring of corruption cases to ensure that judges do not deliver judgments that are at variance with the evidence on the ground due to one form of technicality or another in the statute books.

It will also make it difficult for judges to accept any form of financial inducement from corrupt individuals in order to deliver wrong judgment.

Justice Ayo Salami was suspended on August 8, 2011 for nine months by the NJC after he refused to apologize to the council and former CJN Justice Aloysius Katsina-Alu after a panel of the council found him to have lied against the CJN. But that was the official line. The truth was that Justice Salami was suspended for presiding over a court that sacked four Peoples Democratic Party Governors in Edo, Ondo, Ekiti and Osun. He was about to deliver another judgment against the PDP in Sokoto State when the then CJN Justice Katsina-Alu intervened and told him not to as the impending judgment had been leaked. The rest is history as there were accusations and counter-accusations which eventually led to his suspension. He never regained the seat even when the new CJN Justice Dahiru Musdapher cleared him of all wrongdoing.

Justice Salami's second coming is therefore a triumph to integrity, truth and justice. It will also inspire other Nigerians holding public offices to handle it with integrity, truth and fairness, knowing that no matter what befalls them, posterity will be kind to them.

October 9, 2017.

THE ANTI-NGO BILL

It is with utmost sadness and dismay that millions of Nigerians received the news about the Non-Governmental Organization Regulation and Coordination Bill which has passed Second Reading in the House of Representatives.

The Bill according to its sponsor Mr. Buba Jubril (APC, Kogi) who is also the Deputy Majority Leader of the House of Representatives, seeks to create an NGO Regulatory Commission which will be headed by an Executive Secretary and a 17 member governing board appointed by the President for a five year tenure. According to him (Jubril), *"The bill is primarily to set up a commission to regulate their activities and provide a platform for robust relationships between them and the government for the interest of Nigerians. It will also curb the excesses of NGOs as it will regulate their finances and how they spend money. It will curb terrorism as many NGO's in the North East are currently used as fronts to finance terrorist activities. Churches, Mosques, Esusu and all religious organizations are not the targets of this bill as they are not NGO's".*

Critics of the bill however, think otherwise. The move is seen as an attempt by the National Assembly to asphyxiate the Civil Society for daring to demand probity and accountability from the lawmakers. The recent moves by the Adetokunbo Mumuni led Socio-Economic Rights and Accountability Project (SERAP) and other civil society groups to unearth the salaries and allowances of the lawmakers is a pointer to the negative reaction against NGOs by the National Assembly. Let us not forget that this is not the first time that they are behaving in this manner.

The 8th National Assembly is known for using its legislative power against its supposed enemies. When they were been criticized in the social media by Nigerians for their indulgent lifestyle in the midst of grinding poverty among the citizenry, they reacted by coming up with the anti-social media bill. When INEC wanted to begin the process of recall for one of their own, Senator Dino Melaye, they summoned the INEC Chairman Professor Mahmud Yakubu to come and give an account of his stewardship in a government agency that he retired from years ago. They have also summoned several government officials for criticizing their policies and corrupt tendencies.

I totally and unequivocally condemn the latest move by the National Assembly. This is because this bill if passed into law has the capacity to not only chase away foreign NGOs from Nigeria but also to discourage local ones thereby slowing the pace of our development. Development in this instance being political and economic development. One of the cardinal ingredients in measuring the democratic credentials of a country is the ability of its government to be accountable to the people.

How can the government be accountable to the people if we do not have effective Civil Society Organizations? And how can CSO's be effective if they are being regulated by the very people that they are supposed to hold to account? Giving the power to regulate and issue licenses to NGO's to a regulatory body whose members are appointed by the government simply means that what SERAP and other NGOs are currently doing cannot be done as their licenses would simply be revoked in order to keep their mouths shut.

The ultimate loser will be the Nigerian people. We must not forget the role played by these CSOs to end military rule in this country and bring about the current democracy which the lawmakers are currently enjoying. What this bill seeks to achieve unbeknownst to the lawmakers is the massive underdevelopment of the country. Several NGOs both local and international are making critical inputs into vital areas of the economy.

Take the area of health for example; the fact that Antiretroviral drugs are free today in our hospitals is due to these NGOs. They also carry out health campaigns in schools, rural areas and even urban areas to sensitize the people about certain diseases and how to avoid contacting them or spreading them. It was due to the activities of these NGOs that the AIDS pandemic which at a point in time threatened to reduce the population significantly was curtailed and brought under control.Nigerians must rise up and condemn this bill because if it is passed into law, It will lead to the dictatorship of the politicians over the people and the massive underdevelopment of our nation. What the Military Generals could not achieve through the front door would have been achieved by our politicians through the back door.

October 29, 2017.

RETURN OF MAINA

It came as a rude shock to many when news filtered in last week that the ex-chairman of the Presidential Task Force on Pension Reforms, Mr. Abdulrasheed Abdullahi Maina had not only returned to the country but had also been reinstated back into the civil service with a promotion to boot. The news made many ears tingle and many tongues wag not just because Mr. Maina returned to the country but because it looked like he was being rewarded for the alleged acts of corruption he was said to have committed while in office. It was a big dent on the image of the government especially in its widely acclaimed war against corruption.

Mr. Abdul-Rasheed Maina fled the country in 2013 after an overwhelming public out-cry and repeated attempts by the National Assembly (both arms) including the Economic and Financial Crimes Commission to probe his management of the pension funds in the country. Mr. Maina was alleged to have committed fraud in his management of the pension funds to the tune of several billions of naira.

Some news reports put it is as high as N400 billion naira. He was said to have lived a luxurious lifestyle allegedly with public funds owning two bullet proof cars and spending as much as N8million naira on policemen and other security officials that protect him every two weeks. He was also alleged to have spent over N1billion naira on biometric verification of workers with nothing to show for it.

Various politicians, groups, stakeholders, the media and civil society organizations have roundly condemned Maina's return and subsequent promotion to the post of Director in the civil service including his secondment to the Ministry of Interior. I must also not fail to commend the immediate and prompt response of President Muhammadu Buhari with his directive to the Head of the Civil Service, Mrs. Winifred Eyo-Ita, to immediately relieve Maina of his appointment. It is a step in the right direction. I must also commend his directive to the various security agencies to not only arrest Maina but to charge him to court for his alleged acts of corruption.

He should also take it a step further by instituting a panel of inquiry to investigate how Maina got into the country, and who was responsible for his re absorption and subsequent promotion in the civil service. All those complicit in this disastrous and shameful act should have disciplinary action instituted against them no matter how powerful or highly placed they might be.

November 1, 2017.

ON THE MALABU SCANDAL

The announcement made last week by the Attorney General of the Federation and the Minister of Justice, Mr. Abubakar Malami at an event in Abuja that the British government had returned to the Nigerian government $85 million dollars out of the looted funds in the shady Malabu Oil bloc deal is a welcome development. The Federal Government must however not rest on its oars as it must go the whole hog in unraveling all those involved in what many have dubbed as the largest organized crime in the whole of Africa. It must also go ahead to prosecute them in court and recover every single kobo that was looted by these greedy and unpatriotic elements.

It all started in 1998 when the then Head of State, General Sani Abacha decided to increase indigenous participation in the upstream sector of the petroleum industry. Malabu Oil and Gas owned by the then Petroleum Minister, Chief Dan Etete acquired OPL 245 for $20 million dollars but only made a part payment of $2 million dollars. OPL 245 is an oil field in the Niger Delta that is estimated to hold nine billion barrels of crude oil worth about half a trillion dollars thereby making it one of the largest and most lucrative oil blocs in Africa. Malabu brought in Shell as technical partners but the deal was revoked by Chief Olusegun Obasanjo upon assumption of office in 1999.

He thereafter proceeded to award the oil bloc to Shell without a public bidding which led to a lengthy court battle between Malabu and Shell before they finally agreed on an out of court settlement. Obasanjo, however returned OPL 245 in 2006 to Malabu. Shell began negotiating directly with Etete in order to acquire OPL 245 shortly after Jonathan assumed power in 2010. Jonathan was a tutor to Etete's children when Etete was Minister of Petroleum under Abacha. The deal between Etete and Shell was consummated in 2011 when Malabu sold OPL 245 to Shell and Eni for a whopping $1.1 billion dollars. The Nigerian government under Jonathan acted as intermediaries in the sale since such a huge amount of money could not be paid directly to Etete who was a convicted felon in France as at that time. He had earlier been convicted in absentia of money laundering in France. However, he was given a State pardon by the French authorities in 2013. Shell and Eni paid $1.1 billion dollars to the Government of Nigeria who subsequently transferred $800 million dollars to Malabu.

The transfer was authorized by the then Attorney General of the Federation Mr. Muhammed Adoke and Mr. Yerima Ngama, the then Minister of State for Finance. Malabu transferred over half of the $80 million dollars it received to several accounts around the world as bribes to politicians in Nigeria who helped facilitate the deal. Politicians who have been allegedly fingered in this deal include Former President Olusegun Obasanjo, Former President Goodluck Jonathan, Mohammed Abacha, son of the late maximum dictator and Head of State, General Sani Abacha, the former Attorney General of the Federation Mr. Muhammed Adoke and the Former Minister of Finance, Mr. Yerima Ngama.

There are three main issues involved in this messy oil deal which some have aptly tagged Malabugate. One, that OPL 245 was sold to Malabu Oil in 1998 for a mere pittance. It was sold for $20 million dollars out of which it only paid $2 million dollars. This was for an oil bloc worth several hundreds of billions of dollars. Also, Dan Etete's award of an oil bloc to a company in which he had substantial interest smacks of nothing but corruption.

Two, that the Government of Nigeria under President Jonathan helped transfer such a humongous amount of money to a company owned by a convicted felon in France who bought a valuable national asset at a give-away price beggars belief. All the government officials complicit in this deal should be brought to book, no matter how powerful or highly placed they might be. Three, the Nigerian government only paid $800 million dollars to Malabu Oil leaving a balance of over $200 million dollars. What happened to the remaining $200 million dollars?

These three main issues should be the focus areas of the government as they investigate, prosecute and recover the looted funds in the Malabu Oil deal. Otherwise, it is not yet Uhuru.

November 1, 2017.

WINNING THE ANTI-GRAFT WAR

Corruption is the cankerworm that has eaten deep into the fabric of development in Nigeria. Every day we hear reports of one government official or another involved in graft often to the tune of millions of dollars and sometimes billions. According to the United Kingdom's Department for International Development (DFID), in a report released in 2007, Nigeria's political leaders have stolen about $400 billion dollars between 1960 and 2007.

Corruption is so endemic in Nigeria that in the year 2000, Transparency International rated Nigeria as the most corrupt country in the world. This is in spite of the fact that successive governments in Nigeria since 1983 have declared one form of war on corruption or another in order to stop this hydra headed monster that has stymied the growth and development of this nation.

The question is *How do we ensure that the current anti-graft war being waged by the Muhammadu Buhari-led administration does not go the way of others which ended in failure?'*

First and foremost, we should realize that ending corruption in Nigeria is a collective effort and we are all foot soldiers in the war. We cannot afford to leave it to only the EFCC or the government agencies alone. The current whistle blower policy is a plus to the current anti-graft war as it has emboldened many hitherto timid Nigerians to expose corrupt Nigerians wherever they abound.

It is only reasonable for the executive to send it as a bill to the legislature so that it can become an Act of Parliament thereby making it legal and difficult for subsequent administrations to change. Also, we should avoid acts of corruption in our daily lives as citizens because it is the follower ship that produces the leadership and not vice-versa. Let us not forget that many of our political leaders that we accuse of corrupt acts today were private citizens some 20 years ago.

A situation whereby governors own private jets and have as much as a hundred cars in their fleet does not augur well for us or show good example to the citizens as many now think that public office is all about enjoyment and not service. We should borrow a leaf from the United States where the Secretary of Health and Human Services, Dr. Thomas Price was recently forced to resign for using private jets for official travel instead of commercial airlines.

The judiciary should be strengthened through the creation of special courts to try corruption cases and the cases should be dispensed with within a time frame of six months. The National Orientation Agency should embark on a nationwide campaign to sensitize Nigerians on the nexus between corruption and poverty. The reason why majority of Nigerians still hero-worship corrupt individuals in the society is because of their inability to make the connection between the two. The NOA should partner with the media and also carry out their campaigns mostly in the rural areas were ignorance, illiteracy and poverty is rampant.

Finally, religious leaders should ensure that they preach the truth at all times and not focus on earthly and material achievements alone. They should emphasize spiritual values like love, honesty, integrity, faithfulness, etc. over and above the acquisition of earthly and material possessions. If we are to believe the words of the great German philosopher Karl Marx when he opined that *"Religion is the opium of the masses"*, then we can understand the great power of religious leaders over the masses of the Nigerian people. They should use their power constructively for national gain and not personal gain.

November 2, 2017.

BEFORE RESTRUCTURING

It has become a fad among Nigerian politicians of late to join the populist bandwagon by trumpeting the call for the restructuring of the country. Failed politicians, corrupt politicians, political buccaneers, political profiteers and all sorts of selfish personalities now feel that they can suddenly redeem their image in the eyes of the Nigerian people by calling for the restructuring of the nation. But we cannot be fooled anymore. While I am definitely not against restructuring, I believe that we should not be fooled into thinking that the moment President Muhammadu Buhari restructures the political system, all our problems will just vanish into thin air and we will suddenly find ourselves in the promised land. There are certain hurdles that need to be cleared before we can now begin to advocate for the restructuring of the country in order to make it a truly federal both in word and indeed.

To begin with, the restructuring which most stakeholders have called for should not blind us to the fact that we once practiced true and fiscal federalism in the First Republic. The various regions that made up the federation then were truly independent and had control over their own resources. But most people also forget that it promoted ethnicity, strife, nepotism which eventually led us into a 30-month fratricidal civil war. This means that it ended in a failure. Also, we have tried several political systems in this country and none has been able to take us to Eldorado. We have tried federalism, parliamentary, constitutional monarchy (1960-1963), confederation (which was the trigger for the civil war), military rule, democracy, diarchy (under

Babangida), yet all of these political experiments did not bring us much fruit. What is the guarantee that if the President decides to heed the call of the politicians and restructure the country that Nigeria will suddenly become a great and prosperous nation? I dare say that there is none.

I strongly believe that the call for restructuring of the country is not a genuine one. Why was the call not made during the administration of former President Goodluck Jonathan? Most of the people making the loudest noises today were political office holders in the Jonathan administration yet they made no efforts to restructure the country while in power. Their mouths were shut because they were busy eating the national cake and now that there is no cake to eat they are now whining so that the country can be restructured and they can continue the eating of the cake at the local and regional level where they and their cronies still hold power. Some of them were past military rulers who enacted decrees that made us the quasi-federal structure that we are today yet they shamelessly talk about restructuring and proceed to give instructions on how it should be carried out. For others, it is a political buzzword which they need to win elections in 2019.

Restructuring of the country into a truly federal state will give great economic and political power to the states. There is a critical question which advocates of restructuring are overlooking. That question is "Are our governors sensitive enough to the awesome powers that will be theirs when Nigeria is eventually restructured? Take the issue of state police for example. Imagine what would happen between the Ekiti State governor and the President or between ex-Governor Rotimi Amaechi and former President Goodluck Jonathan. There would have been a bloodbath on the streets of Ado Ekiti and Port Harcourt because of political squabbles between these politicians.

I concur totally with the assertion by former President Olusegun Obasanjo that what we need is the restructuring of the mind and not the restructuring of the nation. It is the people who make a nation great and not vice versa. This is also buttressed by the fact that there are only 16 federal republics in the world of which Nigeria is one yet with the exception of the United States and Germany, most of them are developing countries while there are over 100 unitary states in the world and many of them are developed countries.

The problem is not with the system but with the people. Let us embrace spiritual values of love, honesty, truth and integrity and shun vices like corruption, nepotism, hate speech and tribalism. We should be loyal to our country and patriotism should be our watchword most especially among the youths. Let us not engage in acts that will be beneficial to us and harmful to the nation. It is only after the restructuring of the mind and the embrace of true spiritual values like sacrifice and selflessness by a majority of Nigerians that political restructuring can succeed. Otherwise, it is but an effort in futility.

November 2, 2017.

STILL ON RETURN OF MAINA

The return of the controversial ex-head of the Presidential Task Force on Pension Reforms, Mr. Abdul-Rasheed Abdullahi Maina into the country has ignited a firestorm of revelations which has threatened to not only consume prominent members of the Muhammadu Buhari administration but also the President himself.

President Muhammadu Buhari had asked for a report on the issue to be submitted to him by the Head of the Civil Service of the Federation, Mrs. Winifred Oyo-Ita on the circumstances surrounding Maina's absorption and promotion to the post of Director in the civil service. She has submitted the report to the President. The President speaking through his Special Adviser on Media, Mr. Femi Adesina on a television programme said that the report had come in and promised that the matter would not be swept under the carpet.

But Mr. Maina has not being silent. In an interview he granted a television station whose video is currently trending online, he said that he is being subjected to relentless persecution and media trial because he stopped pension thieves from stealing N5.32 billion naira monthly from the office of the Head of Service and the Police Pension Office. He also said he was shot five times in a bullet proof car which Former President Goodluck Jonathan gave to him in 2013 and that was the reason why he fled the country. His family has also risen stoutly in his defense. They say that their son is not a thief and that he was brought back into the country by agents of the Muhammadu Buhari administration to continue the good work he left unfinished in 2013. They claimed that the houses seized by the Economic and Financial Crimes Commission were houses built by Maina's father long before Maina was born and so could not have been bought with the proceeds of crime. Furthermore, posters of Maina have surfaced in Abuja signifying his intention to contest the gubernatorial election in Borno in 2019. This seems to be a calculated ploy by either Maina or his acolytes to create a whole new dimension to this debacle which is that he is being persecuted because of his political ambitions.

Oyo-Ita's leaked memo to the President which indicates that the President not only had prior knowledge but also ordered Maina's reabsorption and promotion in the civil service is a knotty issue. The million dollar question is *"Would the President investigate himself since he has publicly feigned ignorance of the whole issue? If not, then who would investigate the President?"* Peradventure, the President is found culpable, can any disciplinary measures be instituted against him? The answers to these questions are better imagined.

The supporters of the President can easily give the defense line that Oyo-Ita's memo was doctored. Or that Abba Kyari, the President's Chief of Staff who received the memo on behalf of the President was in actuality acting independent of the President and not on his behalf. That is actually a possibility considering that we are still a country of strong men and not strong institutions. Oyo-Ita's leaked memo also revealed that she briefed Buhari verbally about the implications of the reinstatement of Maina especially the damaging impact on the anti-corruption war of the administration. But she failed to tell us what Buhari's reaction was or if he said anything in response in her memo.

Also, the Attorney General of the Federation, Mr. Abubakar Malami claimed that he acted purely in national interest. He needs to tell us what that national interest is. These and many more are the questions agitating the minds of Nigerians concerning the Maina case and the President needs to move fast in order to lay to rest these issues if he still wants to retain public confidence in his administration's anti-graft war.

November 3, 2017.

MARGINALIZATION CRY

I find it difficult to comprehend how from time to time we hear the cry of marginalization from one ethnic group or another in this country. This is because those who should be crying of marginalization are not the ones crying while those who should not be crying are currently the ones crying. But the truth remains that we have all been marginalized in one way or the other by the ruling class in this country.

It beats my imagination to hear people utter statements like, *"the Igbos are the most marginalized ethnic group in this country"*. This thinking is obviously borne out of a poor knowledge of Nigeria's history or an attempt to live in self-denial. Since the introduction of the elective principle in 1922 with the adoption of the Cliffords Constitution which paved the way for elections in 1923 into the Lagos City Council, the Igbos had a near commanding control of the enterprise called Nigeria.

They produced Nigeria's first indigenous Governor General, first Senate President, first President, first Republican President all in the person of the inimitable Owelle of Onitsha, Dr Benjamin Nnamdi Azikiwe. They also produced the second Senate President in the person of Dr Nwafor Orizu. Jaja Nwachuku became Nigeria's first Speaker of the House of Representatives, the first Permanent Representative to the United Nations and the first Minister of Foreign Affairs. Major General Johnson Thompson Umunnakwe became not only the first indigenous Head of the Army but also Nigeria's first military Head of State. 3 out of the 5 battalion commanders in Nigeria at that time were from the Eastern Region including Lieutenant Colonel Chukwuemeka Odumegwu Ojukwu who was the commander of the 5th Battalion in Kano.

They also held strategic positions in the Army like Quartermaster general, head of Intelligence Unit, Armory, Signals Corp e.t.c. In the academia, the produced 3 Vice-Chancellors out of the 4 existing Universities that we had at that time including the University of Lagos and the University of Ibadan. Igbos won elections in Lagos in pre-independence Nigeria and if not that the late sage Chief Obafemi Awolowo employed the wisdom of the gods, an Igbo man would have been the first Premier of the Western thereby giving them control of 2 out of the 3 regions in Nigeria. Other accomplishments of the Igbos include domination of the federal civil service, the first black man to be appointed as a World Court Judge, first Commonwealth Gold Medalist, richest black man in the world and control of the commanding heights of the economy through the ownership of business enterprises with global acclaim. But all that was to change in the wee hours of January 15th, 1966.

The coup and counter-coup of 1966 led to a chain of events that eventually culminated in a 30-month fratricidal civil war which the Igbos lost. The victors of the war which was the Hausa/Fulani in alliance with the Yorubas became the new hegemons in Nigeria's political life. With the exception of General Olusegun Obasanjo and Chief Ernest Shonekan, the Hausa/Fulani produced 8 leaders (both military and civilians) who governed the nation for about 30 years in quick succession. They created states and local governments which favoured the North. They also changed the principle of allocation of funds to the federating units from the derivation principle to base on population and size of the states. They ran a unitary system concentrating power at the center. They also dominated the security agencies such that Hausa language became the de facto lingua franca of the Army.

The return to democracy in 1999 heralded a new dawn in Nigeria's political life. Chief Olusegun Obasanjo. The new President was said to be totally devoid of ethnic or tribal bias as he won votes in all regions of the country except in his own region where he lost to his opponent

Chief Olu Falae. But we cannot deny certain facts. The heads of the Police and the DSS throughout his 8 year tenure were Yorubas. The Central Bank Governor, the GMD of NNPC and other sensitive positions in Nigeria were allocated to his kinsmen. He also appropriated the office of the Minister of Petroleum to himself throughout his tenure in office. Through some strange shenanigans, Ondo state suddenly became an oil producing state and he proceeded to domicile a multi-billion dollar gas project there. The Niger-Delta people cried out about marginalization but nothing much was done to appease them other than a few acts of tokenism.

If the truth is to be told, there is no geo-political zone that has not produced a President in Nigeria. The South West produced Obasanjo and Shonekan (Ogun State). The South East produced Azikiwe and Aguiyi Ironsi (Anambra and Abia). The South-South produced Goodluck Ebele Jonathan (Bayelsa). The North Central produced Yakubu Gowon (Plateau State), Ibrahim Babangida and Abdulsalami Abubakar (Niger State). The North West produced Umar Musa Yar'adua, Muhammadu Buhari (Both men are from Katsina State) and Murtala Muhammed (Kano State) while the North East produced Sani Abacha (His father is from Borno while his mother is from Kano). Therefore, it is safe to say that no geo-political zone has been truly marginalized. But the same cannot be said of ethnic nationalities.

Many minority ethnic groups like the Urhobo, Efik, Edo,Etche, Igala, Idoma to mention a few have never produced Nigeria's President. Are we saying that these ethnic groups lack presidential materials? Are they doomed to eternal servitude in the Nigerian state just because of their small numbers? These are the people who should be crying about marginalization and not Hausa, Igbo or Yoruba who have benefited from the Nigerian enterprise at one time or the other. Moreover, I believe that the time has come when the oppressed Nigerian masses will rise up as a collective and say no to the oppressive political class in Nigeria who like to dress themselves in the garb of various ethnic colourations so as to deceive the oppressed masses. The only marginalization that i know of is the marginalization of the oppressed Nigerian people by the ruling corrupt political elite.

November 6, 2017.

RUSSIA, TRUMP, AND ELECTION MEDDLING

After the fall of the Soviet Union in 1991, the Russian Federation was born. Elections were held in 1992 and Boris Yeltsin became the first President of the new republic. It was the successor state to the old Union of Socialist Soviet Republic (USSR) which had broken up largely due to the policies of glasnost (openness) and perestroika (restructuring) implemented by the last leader of the Soviet Union, Mr. Mikhail Gorbachev. The new republic inherited the nuclear weapons stockpile of the dismembered the USSR thereby making it one of the most powerful nations in the world but it also inherited the financial woes of the old republic. It received a lot of financial aid from America totaling about $500 billion dollars in order for it to regain its footing financially and more importantly to prevent the country from falling into the hands of extremists who wanted to return the country to the old order.

Circa 2000, an obscure former intelligence officer cum politician rises to power as President. His name is Vladmir Putin. He came to power overwhelmingly aided by his political benefactor and mentor, Boris Yeltsin. However, he had an agenda different from that of Yeltsin in mind and no sooner had he been sworn into office did he break ties with Yeltsin and began to implement his own agenda. His agenda was to restore the lost glory of the defunct Soviet Union now represented by Russia. Putin has dominated Russian politics since becoming President in the year 2000. He has been President for two terms, Prime Minister for one term and now he is President again. His goal is to expand Russia's influence globally. In 2008, during the Russo-Georgian war, Russian forces occupied South Ossetia and Abkhazia which were formerly regions under Georgia following a massive deterioration of relations between Russia and the western-backed government of Georgia. Under the prodding of Russia, these regions later proclaimed their independence from Georgia. He proceeded further to annex Crimea from Ukraine in 2014. Also, the armed conflict in Donbass region of Ukraine which has led to the declaration of independence by the separatist forces of the self-declared Donetsk Peoples Republic and Luhansk Peoples Republic is also a further indication of Mr Putin' thirst for foreign glory. However, it must be said that Russia's intervention in the Syrian civil war has helped the Syrian government to reclaim territories from ISIS and other terrorist groups operating in the country. What other proof of President Putin's power and glory do we need?, than the fact that for four years running, he has been ranked by Forbes magazine as the most powerful man in the world.

Before entering politics, Donald Trump was a successful businessman and television personality. He was fondly referred to as the King of Manhattan due to his dominance of the real estate business in that city. His voyage into politics and subsequent declaration to run for President elicited mixed reactions from several quarters due to some of his outlandish and ambitious policies. Due to a combination of luck and good fortune, he won the Presidential ticket of the Republican Party and went on subsequently to win the Presidential elections. He has however been under intense scrutiny and lately investigation into whether he colluded with the Russians in order to defeat his rival Hillary Clinton at the polls. But most people easily forget that Hillary Clinton had a huge credibility deficit going into that election. That she was already under investigation by the FBI for the use of a private server during her tenure as Secretary of State under Obama.

Her social policies which were identical to that of Obama was a huge turn off to evangelicals and social conservatives. Trump's policies appealed to several groups in America. Social conservatives, fiscal conservatives, the middle class, white collar workers, evangelicals and other religious groups, small business owners and the ultra-right which all coalesced together to send Donald Trump to the White House. Since becoming President, Trump has tried unsuccessfully to implement many of his campaign promises notably the travel man on some Muslim-majority nations, the building of a border wall with Mexico and the repeal and replacement of the Affordable Care Act also known as Obamacare. His efforts to implement these policies have largely been thwarted by Congress and the courts. Only in the area of domestic economics has Trump fulfilled his promise to voters as his administration has created over a million jobs since coming to power in January this year.

Meddling in other countries elections is a violation of International Law. In 1965, the United Nations General Assembly reaffirmed this with a resolution stating: *"No state has the right to intervene, directly or indirectly, for any reason whatever in the internal affairs of any other state"*. According to Wikileaks, America has interfered in 81 foreign elections not including coups between 1946 and 2000. That is why I find it hypocritical when Americans make so much noise about the Russian interference in the last Presidential elections.

People forget that the Russians did not help Trump to win the Republican Presidential ticket and also that Hillary Clinton went into that election with a lot of baggage. The Russians only helped to expose the dark side of her. From time immemorial, nations have always interfered in the affairs of other nations. This is often in order to preserve its interest in that nation no matter how parochial or sinister that interest may be. It is an unwritten norm in international relations between nations and America is not innocent of this illegality.

Mueller's investigation is a waste of time and an unnecessary distraction to President Trump. Trump is an intelligent man who knows how to cover his tracks very well (assuming he is guilty). Don't forget that he has successfully navigated the shark infested waters of the real estate business in New York. He successfully escaped the filing of his tax returns which is a practice that though unwritten has become the norm for every American President.

He also appointed his son-in law and daughter to positions in his government despite cries about the violation of anti-nepotism laws. The investigation might succeed in indicting those around Trump but he will always come out unscathed till the end of his tenure whether in

2020 or 2024. This is because his own party members are afraid to move against him because they do not want to lose their seats in congress. This was unlike the case of Former President Bill Clinton during the Monica Lewinsky trial when it was his own party men that moved against him.

November 6, 2017.

ANAMBRA GUBER

Anambra state is currently the cynosure of all eyes as the race towards the November 18th 2017 gubernatorial elections in the state heats up. There are pretenders and contenders to the throne in a state which has produced several illustrious sons and daughters both locally and internationally. There are four main contenders to the throne and this piece aims to examine their strengths, weaknesses and opportunities. They are Governor Willie Obiano, Dr. Tony Nwoye, Mr. Oseloka Obaze and Chief Osita Chidoka.

Incumbent Governor Willie Obiano of the All Progressives Grand Alliance who is seeking reelection claims he is the man to beat in this election. His greatest achievement is the prompt payment of salaries, pensions and gratuities to government workers, retirees and pensioners as at when due specifically on the 25th of every month. He claims that he took over a state ridden with criminals and violent crimes which discouraged investments and modern development. That he has attracted investments both locally and internationally to the state to the tune of several millions of dollars. He promised to build an airport and further increase the salaries of civil servants in the state if he is reelected for a second term. However, the opposition dispute most of his claims.

They say that the days when Anambra was riddled with criminals and violent crimes was during the turbulent years of the misrule of the Peoples' Democratic Party in the state which ended in 2006 upon the assumption of office by former governor Peter Obi. Ironically, Peter Obi who came to power on the platform of APGA is now campaigning for the return of PDP to the Anambra State Government House. They further claim that Anambra under Obiano had generated a lot of resources even in a time of national economic recession. They ask him what he has done with N445 billion naira which is a combination of federal allocations plus the Internally Generated Revenue of the state (N1 billion naira every month), N75 billion naira in savings which he inherited from Obi's government, N20 billion naira local government funds, N13 billion naira Paris Club Refund and N60 billion naira in foreign and domestic loans as there is no commensurate infrastructure on ground to justify the expenditure of such gargantuan resources in the state. Also, the decline in education in the state which is reflected in the drop in rankings by WAEC and NECO from number one to number six and seven respectively is a chink in Obiano's armour as he battles other political gladiators in the gubernatorial contest.

Dr. Tony Nwoye, the candidate of the All Progressives Congress is the current member representing Anambra East/West Federal constituency in the House of Representatives which incidentally also happens to be Governor Obiano's constituency. His antecedents as the President of the National Association of Nigerian Students and as a member of the Federal House of Representatives not only speaks volumes but also stand him in good stead to be the next governor of the state. It is to his credit that we have the inclusion of the rehabilitation of the Enugu-Onitsha highway which had fallen into a huge state of disrepair in recent times in the 2017 national budget. Also, when the work was abandoned mid-way by contractors, he boldly requested the then Acting President, Professor Yemi Osinbajo to order the contractors back to site which the acting President promptly obliged him. His main weakness is the platform he intends to use to actualize his mandate. The APC is viewed unfavourably by many Igbos due to alleged marginalization by the Buhari government.

Henry Oseloka Obaze is a retired diplomat who worked with both the Nigerian government and the United Nations. He previously served as the Secretary to the State government under former governor Peter Obi and the current Governor Willie Obiano before resigning his appointment in 2016. He is the candidate of the Peoples' Democratic Party. He has promised to invest the state's huge resources in the areas of infrastructure, education and healthcare. While he stands a good chance of emerging as governor due to his integrity, high level of education and international exposure, the factionalization of his party at the state level might work against him as no General goes into battle with a divided army.

Chief Osita Chidoka is the candidate of the United Progressive Party. The UPP manifesto supports the right to self-determination of all ethnic nationalities in Nigeria. This explains the party's ideological support for the Biafran struggle. The party also enjoys widespread support in the hinterland of the state. Chief Chidoka, a former Corp Marshall of the Federal Road Safety Corp and a former Minister of Aviation is a man of unblemished integrity who is unencumbered by corruption cases despite his occupation of two high political offices. He has promised to invest in infrastructure, ICT, ensure better financial management of the state's resources, bring a breath of fresh air to governance and statecraft, and to restore the voice of the Igbos in Nigeria, if he is elected as governor. His main weakness is that he is an ideological politician in a society where it is almost anathema to be one. He also lacks a deep pocket to enable him match the spending of his rivals on the hustings.

As Anambrarians go to the poll on the 18th of this month, one of these men will emerge as Governor. Their personal strengths and weaknesses will not only determine the direction the state will go in the next four years but ultimately the destiny of the state.

November 9, 2017.

SENATE AND EXCESS CRUDE ACCOUNT

The recent moves by the Nigerian Senate to abolish the Excess Crude Account is worrisome and an unwelcome development. It is a step in the wrong direction and totally out of tandem with the wishes, yearnings and aspirations of the Nigerian people.

In a motion titled *"The Excess Crude Account: An Illegality and a Drain Pipe"* sponsored by Senator Rose Oko (Cross River, North) and 42 others, they requested the Executive to act in conformity with sections 80 (1-4) and sections 162 (1-3) of the 1999 constitution as amended which stipulates that all revenues accruing to the Federal Government should be paid into the Federation Account. They further stated that the Excess Crude Account was an illegality since it is unknown to law and urged the Executive to pay the amount above the oil benchmark into the Federation Account while it appropriates a portion of the fund to the Sovereign Wealth Fund.

The Excess Crude Account was set up in 2004 by former President Olusegun Obasanjo to provide savings for the country and stabilization for the economy during periods of shortfall in oil revenue. Accruals to the Excess Crude Account was expected to be the amount above the benchmark of crude oil sales. When Obasanjo left office on May 29th, 2007, he left $25 billion dollars in the ECA and by the end of the year 2007; the account balance in the ECA was a whopping $67 billion dollars

Between 2007 and 2011, when Presidents Yar'adua and Jonathan held sway, the ECA got depleted to less than a billion dollars. The money was shared to all the 36 state governors due to pressure mounted on the President by these governors who claimed that they needed these monies for the infrastructural development of their various states. But there is very little to show for the much talked about infrastructural development in these states as what we see are a litany of decaying and abandoned projects all over the nooks and crannies of Nigeria.

Some of these monies were simply shared among the many political associates, appointees and friends of these governors who promptly transferred these monies to their private bank accounts in Europe and America. Moreover, when the rainy day came as typified in the global crash in oil prices in 2014 which resulted in huge revenue shortages for Nigeria since we run a mono economy heavily dependent on oil, it triggered an economic recession which we are yet to fully recover from. Today, 20 states of the federation are unable to pay workers' salaries and allowances for about a year now.

What the Senate should do is to legalize the ECA through the creation of the relevant laws and regulatory framework with a proviso that half of the money accruable to the ECA should be invested in the Sovereign Wealth Fund. We should not throw away the baby with the bathwater. We need to save for financial contingencies in the future like a fall in the global price of crude oil and also to provide for generations unborn so that in the future when the world's shifts it's attention away from fossil fuels, we do not suddenly become a poor nation overnight begging for aid from other countries in order to survive.

November 10, 2017.

MUCH ADO ABOUT TITHING

Ever since Pastor Enoch Adeboye, the General Overseer of the Redeemed Christian Church of God threw a shade at Cool FM OAP Daddy Freeze over the issue of whether tithing is mandatory for Christians or not and the reply of the MC to the highly revered man of God, the social media has been agog with comments for or against this age-old Christian practice. This piece is not an attempt to justify or repudiate tithing by Christians; that is a job for theologians. Rather, it is an attempt to look at the casus belli of the agitations for the abolition of tithing by some Christians and the roles the church can play in our quest to achieve greatness and prosperity for all in Nigeria.

The critical factor which triggered this debate about tithing is nothing but the lavish and luxurious lifestyle of Nigerian preachers in a time of economic recession. At a time when 80% of the population are living below the poverty line, the news of the recent acquisition of a Private Jet and a Rolls Royce Phantom by Pastor David Ibiyeomie of the Salvation Ministries in Port Harcourt to celebrate his 55th birthday anniversary has left a sour taste in the mouths of many. Majority of the preachers in Nigeria do not have any other source of income other than their total dependence on the tithes and offerings of the faithful. Politicians also face criticism from the people due to their corrupt and lavish lifestyle but theirs is mild compared to preachers because they occupy a tenured position while preachers can be in office till death do them part.

Also, their teachings about tithing and giving have deadened the conscience of many Nigerians towards the poor and vulnerable in the society around them. It is a belief in several African cultures that when you genuinely help the poor and less privileged around you, you would be blessed by God in return. This was what prompted many Africans to embrace the extended family system and to extend a hand to the poor and needy in the society. But today all that has changed.

The Pastors now teach that it is when you pay your tithes that God would bless you and failure to pay it would attract a curse from God. Many people now pay their tithes faithfully to the churches but at the detriment of caring for their parents, siblings and other members of their extended family. We have also heard of several instances of people who steal money in their workplaces and pay the tithe of the money to the church in a bid to attract a blessing to their lives. The non-accountability of Pastors to their members on how the tithes of the members are spent not only leaves a lot to be desired but also ample room for speculations about corruption and embezzlement of tithe funds.

The Church should harp more on spiritual values like love, honesty, sacrifice, brotherhood, integrity, loyalty and patriotism rather than its current focus on prosperity and materialism. We are currently experiencing the gradual destruction of our value system as most Nigerians are determined to become rich at all costs seeing that the corrupt rich are being celebrated as heroes while the honest poor are regarded as villains.

The church should serve as the moral anchor that Nigerians would cling unto in these times of moral and ethical relativity. Also, the church should become socially responsible by giving back to society. The missionaries who came to Nigerian in the 19th century built schools, established newspapers, hospitals and awarded scholarships at practically no cost to the Natives. They did all these with less than 10% of the funds that Nigerian mega-churches are currently controlling.

Church leaders should avoid allying themselves with and endorsing politicians during elections. They should be neutral so as to enable them speak truth to power without fear or favour. Nigerian Churches should emulate their counterparts in other countries where the church is a positive force to be reckoned with politically rather the kowtowing to the whims and caprices of any politician who makes a donation to the church.

The prosperity doctrine of giving and receiving has been grossly misrepresented by the clergy and misunderstood by the laity. Our Pastors should rather dwell on the building blocks of economic prosperity by teaching their members principles like thrift, entrepreneurship, productivity and savings. They should engage in economic empowerment schemes which will benefit the members. They should also invest their surplus earnings in the productive sector of the economy (e.g. Agriculture) which will not only create jobs for their teeming members but will also contribute significantly to the GDP of the nation. They should endeavour to reduce their investment in consumables like expensive automobiles, luxury yachts, private jets, e.t.c as these do not add anything to the Nigerian economy since they are not manufactured here. Rather they take away from our economy as they are often purchased with scarce foreign exchange.

This is a clarion call on the church to curb it's excesses and rise up like a giant to fulfill its role in Nigeria's voyage towards peace, progress and prosperity.

November 13, 2017.

OBASANJO IN THE EYES OF HISTORY

In Africa, we do not celebrate the living but the dead. The biblical statement that a prophet is not without honour except among his own people is only true in Africa because Americans and Europeans are known to venerate their leaders while they are alive and much more when they are dead. But in Africa, it is the exact opposite. We vilify and condemn our leaders when they are alive and then turn around to praise them when they have departed to the great beyond.

This explains why the wartime British Prime Minister, Winston Churchill, has about 6000 biographies written in his honour while great African statesmen like Nkrumah, Mandela, Lumumba and Nasser each have less than ten biographies written in their honour. This piece is an attempt to do a synopsis of the achievements of one of the greatest African leaders of all times, Chief Olusegun Obasanjo while he is still alive so as to dispel wrong notions and misconceptions that those living may have about him and also to serve as a reference material for future generations of Nigerians who will not have the opportunity to have him physically present in their midst.

Chief Olusegun Obasanjo rose to national prominence as a soldier in the Nigerian Army when as the General Officer Commanding of the highly skilled and efficient 3rd Marine Commando, he received the instrument of surrender from the Biafrans thus signaling an end to the Nigerian civil war (1967-1970). He was appointed as Federal Commissioner of works in 1974 by the then Head of State, General Yakubu Gowon with the task of building roads, bridges, highways and other infrastructural facilities in the post war oil-boom era in Nigeria. After General Murtala Muhammed came to power in 1975, Obasanjo became the de facto Vice President of Nigeria in his capacity as the Chief of Staff Supreme Headquarters.

He worked closely with General Muhammed in the formulation and implementation of several policies including the anti-corruption war (which was the first of its kind in post-colonial Nigeria), the purge in the civil service which ensured efficiency and effectiveness and the moral and financial support for radical liberation groups in Africa committed to the decolonization of the African continent.

Obasanjo's initial incarnation as Nigeria's Head of State in 1976 was purely by happenstance due to the gruesome assassination of General Muhammed in a failed coup led by Colonel B.S Dimka and other confederates. He swiftly swung into action by promulgating the Nigerian Enterprises Promotion Decree which encouraged the growth of an indigenous middle class. He made a massive impact in the area of agriculture through his Operation Feed the Nation programme and its attendant creation of several River Basins mostly in Northern Nigeria.

With Soviet assistance, he built the Ajaokuta Steel Complex thus laying a solid foundation for the industrialization of Nigeria. In the petroleum sector, two out of our four existing refineries namely Warri Refinery and Kaduna Refinery were built during his tenure. Obasanjo increased the number of universities in Nigeria from 5 to 13, my alma mater, the University of Port Harcourt being among the newly created universities. He also made primary education in Nigeria free and compulsory through the promulgation of Universal Primary Education. Unity schools a.k.a. Federal Government Colleges were established all over the federation during his tenure as military Head of State. Obasanjo continued his predecessor's support for radical groups all over Africa committed to the decolonization of the continent when he nationalized British Petroleum due to the British government's support for the Apartheid policy in South Africa.

In his second incarnation as civilian President, Obasanjo initiated several policies which set Nigeria on the path of greatness. He introduced the Global System Mobile phones which made telephony services available to the poorest of the poor in a clear defiance of the crude assertion made by a former Minister of Communications when he remarked that *"Telephones are not meant for the poor"*. He introduced Banking reforms which made Nigerian banks stronger, healthier and globally competitive. He created the Niger Delta Development Commission (NDDC) to bring about development in the Niger Delta and the Universal Basic Education Commission (UBEC) to enhance literacy among Nigerians. He increased Nigeria's foreign reserves from $2 billion dollars in 1999 to $43 billion dollars in 2007.

He also created the Excess Crude Account; an account where oil revenues above the benchmark price of crude oil sales in the national budget where paid into. The money in the account was savings meant for the stabilization of the economy during periods of shortfall in oil revenue. The account balance at the end of his tenure in 2007 was a whopping $25 billion dollar. Nigeria's exit from the Paris and London Club of creditors when she received debt forgiveness to the tune of $18 billion dollars was a testament to Chief Obasanjo's international acceptance and love for his country.

Obasanjo is the most recognized, most influential and most respected Nigerian leader globally whether military, civilian, dead or alive. He has worked with several international organizations including the UN, AU, Commonwealth, ECOWAS e.t.c. His list of achievements in diplomacy and international politics are too numerous that I am constrained by space to attempt a listing of all of them. He is the only Nigerian leader to receive 3 US Presidents namely Jimmy Carter, Bill Clinton and George W. Bush during their visits to the country. He is also Nigeria's longest serving ruler with a cumulative total of 11 years in power.

Like all mortals, Chief Obasanjo is not without his flaws and failures. However, it will be a great disservice to his person and the nation at large if we continually dwell on his flaws and failures which when compared to his achievements in office is greatly infinitesimal.

November 15, 2017.

TOM AND JERRY

The recent show of shame which occurred in Port Harcourt when security operatives attached to the Governor of Rivers State, Barrister Nyesom Wike and those attached to the Minister of Transportation and the former governor of the State, Rt. Hon. Rotimi Amaechi, almost had a shoot-out when the convoys of both men clashed on a highway in the city, has only further revealed the character and caliber of politicians holding public office in Nigeria.

I title this piece Tom and Jerry after the cartoon television series which was popular among young children in this country in the 90's. It is a tale of a cat (Tom) and a mouse (Jerry) who are constantly at war with each other over one thing or the other with one not allowing the other to rest. Since Amaechi and Wike parted ways in 2013, both men have succeeded in polarizing everyone and everything in Rivers State including revered institutions like the Church and the Traditional institutions into two camps with incessant attacks and counter-attacks from both camps. The latest is the claim of an assassination attempt by both camps as a result of the recent melee which occurred penultimate weekend.

Both men should be told in clear and unmistakable terms that Rivers State is bigger than both of them. Since this personality clash began some years ago, countless lives have been lost on both sides of the divide due to the inability of both politicians to sheathe their swords and work for the interest of peace in the state. They do not necessarily have to belong to the same party but words, acts, and actions that are inimical to the interest of peace in the state should be avoided by both parties.

The security agencies should avoid being partisan and endeavour to carry out their duties with the highest professional standards and also without fear or favour. The youths should avoid selling their destiny for a morsel of bread by blindly choosing to support one camp or the other since in reality none of the camps are innocent nor do any of them have the interest of the people that they claim to lead at heart. They should remember the popular African adage that says *"When two elephants fight, it is the grass that suffers"*.

November 15, 2017.

A MAD MILLIONAIRE

The exchange of words between some government officials on one hand and some concerned citizens on the other hand about whether the whistle blower in the $43 million dollars Ikoyi-gate scandal has been paid his entitlements or not is a source of great concern to many. Another worrisome dimension was also added to the whole drama with concerns about his mental health being raised which precipitated his forced examination by a mental health specialist. The amount of money to be paid to the whistle blower is about 806 million naira.

It all began when the Chairman of the Economic and Financial Crimes Commission, Mr. Ibrahim Magu fired the initial salvo at an anti-corruption conference in far-away Vienna, Austria when he said that the whistle blower in the Ikoyi-gate scandal who is widely believed to be one of the security men protecting the property has been paid all his entitlements. That statement immediately attracted a rebuttal from Lagos Lawyer and Human Rights Activist, Mr. Femi Falana who promptly debunked the claim by Magu saying he knows the whistle blower in question and that he had not been paid a dime.

Wilson Uwajaren, spokesperson of the EFCC joined the fray when he attempted to clarify Magu's statement by saying what Magu meant was that he would soon be paid by the Ministry of Finance. Mrs. Kemi Adeosun, Nigeria's Honourable Minister of Finance, said they were planning to pay the whistleblower soon and that the delay in payment was caused by bureaucratic bottlenecks. A strange twist was added to the whole saga when Professor Itse Sagay, Chairman of the Presidential Advisory Council on the Anti-Corruption War, claimed that the reason the money had not been paid was to prevent the man from going bonkers and spending the money frivolously due to the fact that he was a poor man who had not encountered such a huge amount of money in his life before. He further stated that the man was under tutoring on how best to spend the money so as not to attract unnecessary attention to himself which might have grave security implications. Meanwhile, the whistle blower's lawyer placed an advertorial in some national dailies and also wrote a letter to the Ministry of Finance intimating them that he is the legal representative of the whistleblower and also of two impostors who are claiming to be the rightful whistleblower.

The ding-dong over whether the whistle blower has been paid or not is actually sending a wrong signal to Nigerians that the whole program is a scam. This portends danger for the government's anti-corruption war as Nigerians with valuable information on the whereabouts of our stolen patrimony might be tempted to lose faith in the program. The Ministry of Finance should straighten out the process of paying whistleblowers through the elimination of bureaucratic bottlenecks which currently impede the process of payment. They should also collect taxes on every amount of money that is paid out to the whistle blower.

It is the prerogative of the whistle blower to spend his money as he deems fit. After all, he is an adult so I do not see any need for tutoring by anyone on how he should spend his newly found fortune. The whole issue of his mental state could have been a misinterpretation of signs of extreme happiness and anxiety to lay his hands on the money so that he can begin to live the good life.

After spending many years if not his entire life in poverty, his behaviour should not seem strange as that is the expected behaviour of anyone in his shoes. Also, the whole drama surrounding the payment of funds to the whistle blower is capable of attracting unnecessary attention to him which could spell doom for him security wise as the looters of the funds are still roaming the streets free. Subsequently, adequate protection should be given to all whistleblowers. They could easily do this by placing them on the watch list of various security agencies for at least a year after their whistle blowing.

Finally, the whistle blower policy should be legalized through an act of parliament so as to ensure that the current anti-corruption war would not be derailed when a new administration comes on board. Government must do everything within its power to get to the bottom of this matter because this issue has the capability of slowing down the anti-corruption train as the whistleblower program is a key component of the current administration anti-graft war.

November 20, 2017.

KADUNA: EL-RUFAI'S BOLD MOVE

The recent move by the Kaduna State Governor, Mallam Nasir El-Rufai to sack about 22,000 primary school teachers in the state who flunked a competency test based on a primary four entry level examination is not only commendable but a step in the right direction. The plan which also involves replacing the sacked teachers with qualified ones who have been thoroughly screened and tested will go a long way in sanitizing the rot in our educational system and saving the future of the next generation.

Over the years, there have been hues and cries by several Nigerians complaining about the rot in our educational sector. Various educational summits have been organized by both private and government institutions seeking a redress of the imbalance and rot bedeviling education in this country. Our Universities now produce graduates who are at best certified illiterates since most of them cannot defend the certificates that they possess. The situation is not different both at the secondary and primary level of education.

Cheating to pass examinations has now become the order of the day resulting in a society with an abundance of certificates but with a low level of knowledge. Most of the teachers that the Governor plans to sack were recruited by past political leaders in the state who saw the education sector as a dumping ground for all shades of characters including supporters, thugs, acolytes, associates, e.t.c in blatant disregard of their aptitude and qualification.

That is why i am stupefied by the opposition from various quarters to the Governor's bold move to cleanse the Augean stable. Most of those opposing the planned sack of the teachers are either doing so out of ignorance of the fact that the sacked teachers would be replaced by qualified teachers which means that there is no increase in the labour market or are doing so out of mischief, malice, blind political opposition or an amalgam of the afore stated reasons.

What they are doing unbeknownst to them is placing sentiments above merit. Many of them have their children schooling overseas or in private schools in this country so they cannot contemplate the level of decay in the education sector. The hypocrisy of the labour unions in Nigeria is openly manifest since they did not deem it fit to carry out protests in over 20 states of the federation that are owing workers' salaries and allowances for over a year now but are quick to respond to a move to replace unqualified teachers with qualified ones in Kaduna.

In the words of the Governor, *"We are not sacking teachers. We are only replacing unqualified people who are unfit to be called teachers to save the future of the next generation"*. Former Governor Adams Oshiomohle of Edo state tried a similar move some years ago when he discovered to his chagrin that a teacher in a secondary school in the state could not read a text in a Literature textbook. However, the soft pedaled on his plan due to widespread opposition and political exigencies. That is why I commend the endorsement of El-Rufai's messianic move by President Muhammadu Buhari. The endorsement by the President will no doubt go a long way in strengthening the hands of the Governor against the hearing voices of his traducers.

November 20, 2017.

PERILOUS SEARCH FOR THE GOLDEN FLEECE

It came as a rude shock to many a few weeks ago when news filtered in that 26 Nigerian dead bodies mostly teenage girls between the ages of 14 and 18 were found in an Italian warship named Cantabria. Subsequent investigations by the Italian authorities revealed that the girls drowned while trying to cross the Mediterranean Sea from Libya to Italy and also that two of the girls were pregnant. They also did not find any sign of sexual molestation or rape on the dead bodies.

However, this is not the first time that this has occurred. As a matter of fact, the success rate is far higher than the failure rate which has only served to encourage many young people to try their luck. According to statistics from the Italian Foreign Ministry, over 100,000 migrants successfully crossed the Mediterranean Sea from Libya to Italy this year alone. What are the factors propelling our youths to embark on such hazardous journeys often through deserts where they could be attacked by bandits or devoured by wild animals looking for food to eat?

They could drown in the Mediterranean while trying to cross from Libya to Italy often on overcrowded dinghies and without life jackets. Who are the sponsors of these youths as recent research indicates that it costs nothing less than $6,000 to ferry these youths to Europe through these dangerous routes? What steps can be taken by the various authorities to stop this illegal migration?

The Nigerian government through the Ministry of Information and the National Orientation Agency in collaboration with the media should embark on a massive sensitization campaign to disabuse the minds of young people about the illusion of prosperity overseas. The current economic hardship bedeviling our nation has made many to falsely assume that you can literally pick up gold from the streets of Europe and America. The campaign should also promote the virtues of self-reliance, hard work and the dignity of labour among the youths.

The youths should be told in clear, unequivocal, unambiguous and unmistakable terms that the days of depending on the government for white collar jobs are over. That it is only through the engaging of your divine and God-given talents that you can be successful in life. One wonders how they are able to raise the princely sum needed to embark on the trip when they complain of economic hardship principally induced by lack of jobs. The same energy that they use in generating such an amount of money can also be used to generate funds which can be invested in productive ventures which will not only benefit them but also the larger society.

The African Union should take proactive steps in not only blocking the smugglers routes but also criminalizing illegal migration with punitive measures for both the smugglers and the illegal migrant. The European Union most especially Italy should stop granting refugee status to those who cross the Mediterranean successfully. They should be immediately deported to their home countries. A similar tragedy occurred some years ago when over 2000 migrants (many of them Nigerians) perished in the Mediterranean Sea close to the Italian Island of Lampedusa while on a perilous voyage to seek the proverbial golden fleece. This is one tragedy too many and all hands must be on deck to forestall a recurrence of this avoidable waste of human capital and future leaders.

November 21, 2017.

MUGABE'S FALL FROM GRACE

Comrade Robert Gabriel Mugabe, Zimbabwe's only ruler since it became a democracy in 1980, and one of Africa's longest serving rulers (37 years in power) finally bowed to pressure and resigned this week as President of the Republic. It was a fitting climax to a series of events which began last week when the military rolled out thanks unto the streets and effectively placed Mugabe under house arrest. It also marked the end of a power struggle within the ruling ZANU-PF party between the G-40 made up of Mugabe's wife, Grace and her allies, and the Lacoste faction which is made up of Former Vice President and current President Emmerson D. Mnangagwa, General Constantino Chiwenga (representing the military) and the war veterans of Zimbabwe's struggle for liberation.

The struggle for power in ZANU-PF actually began in 2014 when the two factions united to oust Former Vice President, Dr. Joyce Mujuru from power. They later turned against each other in a bid to produce Mugabe's successor as the 93 year old leader grew increasingly weak and frail. However, things got to a head when Mugabe sacked Mnangagwa as Vice President citing disloyalty which triggered a chain of events that eventually culminated in his outing from power. But how did Zimbabwe get to this point? Circa 1980, Mugabe came to power as a hero beloved not only by Zimbabweans but by the whole of Africa. He was regarded as a hero, liberator, emancipator and an African statesman. He transmuted from Prime Minister to President and everything went on smoothly for him and the country until Britain repudiated the terms of the Lancaster House Agreement which was signed in 1980. The Lancaster House Agreement stipulated that Britain would pay a certain amount of money to Zimbabwe annually as compensation to enable Zimbabwe redress the inequitable distribution of land in the country. The money would then be given to Black Farmers to buy back land from the White Settler Farmers; land which originally belonged to their ancestors. Everything went on as planned with Britain making the payments annually and Mugabe even receiving a Knighthood from Her Majesty, Queen Elizabeth II until Tony Blair came to power as Prime Minister in 1997 and put an abrupt end to the payments citing lack of finances even when Britain was not known to be experiencing any recession of any sort at that time.

Three years later, under pressure from the war veterans, Mugabe ordered the forced seizure of lands from White Settler Farmers and the redistribution of such lands to the blacks most especially to the war veterans. This attracted sanctions from not only Britain but also from her allies-America and other European countries, which effectively crippled Zimbabwe's economy turning the once breadbasket of Africa into a basket case-apologies to Archbishop Desmond Tutu. Every effort by the West to remove Mugabe from power failed as he enjoyed maximum support from the triad of the party, the military, and the war veterans. But that was until 2014 when his wife Grace who had hitherto remained incognito became increasingly active in public life. Her vaulting ambition to succeed Mugabe as President when he dies is at the heart of the political crisis that has engulfed Zimbabwe since 2014.

As a matter of fact, it will not be wrong to posit that Mugabe's fall from grace was due to his wife Grace as her active involvement in public life including her incendiary statements alienated Mugabe from his power base. A similar situation in the 18th century led to the downfall of a French king and marked the beginning of the French Revolution. We have also had two similar cases in Nigeria, one more recently which led to the downfall of two Nigerian Presidents. Indeed, those who fail to learn from history are doomed to repeat its mistakes.

November 24, 2017.

LESSONS FROM EKWUEME'S LIFE

Former Vice President of Nigeria, Dr. Alex Ifeanyichukwu Ekwueme was a rare gem, a colossus, and one out of a handful of Nigerians who though was an active participant in Nigeria's corrupt political process exited the stage with his integrity unblemished. The late Ide of all Aguata Communities in Anambra State (about 41 kingdoms) exited this corrupt and sinful world to join the saints triumphant on Sunday, the 19th of November, 2017. He was a man of numerous accomplishments. He set up Nigeria's first indigenous Architectural firm - Ekwueme Associates, Architects and Town Planners with 16 offices nationwide out of the then 19 states of the federation. Before then, he was one of the first Nigerians to be awarded a Fulbright Scholarship to study Architecture in America.

Chief Ekwueme achieved so many things in life-professionally, politically and socially. He played pivotal roles in Nigeria's political life most especially during periods of crises. However, his greatest achievement politically was his reign as Nigeria's 5th Vice President in the Second Republic (1979-1983) under former President Shehu Shagari. What are the lessons that the youths most especially the younger generation of politicians in Nigeria can learn from the life of this intellectual juggernaut, professional leviathan and successful politician? If there is anything that stands Chief Ekwueme out among the pack of colorless politicians that currently bestride Nigeria's political space, it is his integrity, consistency and love for the Nigerian people.

Though he was often shabbily treated by successive governments after his inglorious exit from power in 1983 through a military coup and his subsequent incarceration without trial, he bore no grudges against anyone and was ever willing to contribute his quota to the development of the country. Even when the Peoples' Democratic Party which he helped create in 1998 during the regime of the late maximum dictator General Sani Abacha, turned its back on him, he did not defect from the party and remained a life-long member till his death. His love for the downtrodden in the society led him to set up the Alex Ekwueme Foundation which has awarded scholarships to thousands of indigent students to study both at home and abroad. The Foundation has also given out loans to several indigent people to set up businesses of their own.

The former VP shunned the primitive accumulation of wealth through political office which is the hallmark of politicians in Nigeria nay Africa. He was a detribalized Nigerian who played politics without bitterness or rancour. Dr. Ekwueme lived an exemplary life; a life worthy of emulation by the youths and the younger generation of politicians in Nigeria today. He was a living proof that it is possible to insert your feet into the murky waters of Nigerian politics and yet your feet would remain unsoiled. Adieu Chief Alex Ifeanyichukwu Ekwueme.

November 24, 2017.

ATIKU'S UNBRIDLED AMBITION

Former Vice President Alhaji Atiku Abubakar decamped last week from the ruling All Progressives Congress citing Kaduna State Governor Mallam Nasir El-Rufai's leaked memo to the President which highlighted President Muhammadu Buhari's neglect of key stakeholders in the party in the decision making process and in the appointment of key officials as his reason for his departure. The leaked memo to the President also talked about the failure of the party to fulfill its campaign promises two years into the life of the administration. In a swift reaction, Governor El-Rufai responded by saying that the party was aware of his planned defection and that he did it a month earlier. He went further to say that he would not be missed in the party and wished him success in his future endeavors.

Atiku has been trying to be Nigeria's President since 1993 when at the Jos Convention of the Presidential primaries of the defunct Social Democratic Party, he placed a distant third after Dr. Babagana Kingibe and Chief M.K.O Abiola who turned out the eventual winner of the primaries. Before then, he was a senior customs officer and a successful businessman who had amassed a fortune. He was later chosen by Chief Olusegun Obasanjo as his running mate in the 1999 Presidential elections after he had already emerged as the governor-elect of Adamawa state. He served as Nigeria's Vice President under the Presidency of Chief Olusegun Obasanjo from 1999 to 2007.

Atiku, one of the few Nigerian politicians often referred to by his first name, has never hidden his desire to be President of Nigeria. This was the main reason he fell out with his principal, Chief Olusegun

Obasanjo. He seems quite bashful and unapologetic about his ambition to be President as he seems to believe that it is his God-ordained destiny. What the Americans like to call Manifest Destiny. But does Atiku possess the appropriate Presidential credentials even after his 8 year tenure as Vice President? If we are to judge him by his antecedents, can we truly say that he is the best material for the Presidency at this moment in our national life? Will the public's perception of him as a corrupt politician not impede his chances of getting the plum job? Or will Mother luck smile on him and grant him victory on his fifth attempt to be President of Nigeria?

Truth be told, Atiku is not what we need now that Nigeria is slowing joining the comity of nations marching towards the 22nd century. Corruption is a big problem on our hands and the last thing that we need now is a President bogged down by corruption allegations both at home and overseas. We should not get carried away with sentiments. We should take a cue from South Africa where President Jacob Zuma was elected despite corruption allegations against him and the seeming regret of that decision by the electorate.

Also, his lack of ideological politics, policy inconsistencies, and seeming desperation to occupy the office of the President which manifests itself in his serial defection from one party to another does not place him in good stead to occupy the most exalted office in the land. Even if he gets the Presidential ticket of the Peoples' Democratic Party or any other party, there are too many powerful politicians who worked with him in times past waiting in the wings to spill out dark secrets about him which will turn off many prospective voters. Chief Olusegun Obasanjo, his arch-nemesis his bidding his time waiting patiently for 2019 before turning loose his verbal bazooka on him to finally liquidate him politically just like he did to former President Goodluck Jonathan in the 2015 elections. Others who might toe the Obasanjo line include former Minister of Defence, General Theophilous Danjuma and Governor El-Rufai.

Atiku's extension of a hand of fellowship to the youths and the Igbos should be taken with a pinch of salt as he did nothing to elevate the status of both groups when he was in power. This gesture is an afterthought and one of the manifestations of his desperation to get power in order to satisfy his over-bloated ego. My advice to Nigerians is to shine their eyes as we gradually approach 2019. We should not be deceived by Atiku's gimmicks, theatrics and rhetoric.

November 27, 2017.

EFCC/DSS FEUD

The unnecessary rivalry between the Economic and Financial Crimes Commission and the Department of State Services is condemnable and totally uncalled for. This war of supremacy which has been going on for over a year now came to limelight when the DSS issued two security reports signed by a Director in the agency indicting the Chairman of EFCC, Mr. Ibrahim Magu accusing him of corruption and other sundry allegations. The Nigerian Senate relied upon the security reports issued by the DSS to deny the confirmation of Magu as EFCC Chairman.

The President instead of calling both men to order since they are both his appointees and also because they answer directly to him chose to side with Magu mandating him to continue in the office in an acting capacity even though lawyers, lawmakers, public affairs analysts and other stakeholders have given varying interpretations to the EFCC Act as to the legality or illegality of the President's directive. The latest clash between the two agencies is the widely reported refusal of the DSS to allow the EFCC arrest it's immediate past Director-General, Dr. Ita Ekpeyong and also the recently sacked Director-General of the National Intelligence Agency, Ambassador Ayo Oke,

What baffles me is the fact that two different agencies with unrelated duties and mandates could bicker and squabble publicly over issues which are yet to come to public light. Is there personal animus between Magu and Lawal Daura, Director-General of the DSS? If there are personal grievances, is it right for both of them to use the apparatus of state to settle personal scores? Why has the President not intervened to settle the rift between both men just as he did recently in the case between Winifred Oyo-Ita, Head of the Civil Service of the Federation, and Abba Kyari, the Chief of Staff to the President? Is the non-intervention by the President due to the fact that Daura, the DG of the DSS is his nephew? These questions seem somewhat rhetorical as only 3 men have the answers to these questions- Daura, Magu and President Buhari and until such a time that they chose to reveal the answers to these questions, we will perpetually remain in the dark as to the truth of the whole matter.

Inter-agency rivalry most especially in the security sector is not limited to Nigeria alone as we also saw the rivalry between the FBI and the CIA in the US in the aftermath of the 9/11 terrorist attacks. But it was not done in the crude form that we are witnessing between the DSS and the EFCC. The security agencies in the US chose to hoard information from one another so as to create a public perception that they were working optimally thereby placing them in a vantage position to receive a bigger budget from Congress. However, in Nigeria, it is nothing but a crude power play in order to satisfy the over-bloated egos of some power hungry officials.

It is fortuitous that the Nigerian Senate has risen up to the occasion by roundly condemning this show of shame by agencies which are supposed to be working for the interest of Nigerians. Both agencies should focus on their core mandates rather than engaging in trivialities. President Muhamadu Buhari should intervene lest he gives credence to allegations by the Opposition that he is not only weak and ineffective but also that he is not in control of the government. This rivalry is also capable of setting a wrong precedent which some unscrupulous government officials might want to emulate in the future. Finally, the intervention by the President would destroy the myth of a cabal existing in the President and pooh-pooh allegations of nepotism, tribalism, cronyism and clannishness which have dogged the President since his assumption of office in 2015.

November 28, 2017.

ROGUE YOUTH LEADERS

For many decades in Nigeria, there have been widespread clamour for the devolution of power to the youths. Indeed, the youths are said to be the leaders of tomorrow. But 38 years after that famous phrase was uttered by General Olusegun Obasanjo, Nigeria's former Head of State, the youths of Nigeria are yet to lead the country. It can be safely argued that the youths of 1979 have now become men today and are leading the country, but a cursory look at the facts on the ground indicate otherwise.

That General Olusegun Obasanjo, the coiner of that phrase 38 years ago is still an active participant in Nigeria's political process lends credence to my assertion. Mind you, when I talk about leadership, I am not talking about it in its strict sense which is political leadership but in its generic sense or rather permit me to say that I am using the word loosely. Apart from entertainment, sports and social media, there seems to be very few youth leaders making meaningful impact in every sector of our national life. Rather, the youths are bogged down by unemployment and economic hardship which has degenerated into frustration and has made many of them to embrace vices like illicit sex, pornography, gambling, armed robbery, e.t.c.

However, there is an ugly trend which is beginning to gain traction among the political leadership in Nigeria. It is nothing more than the fact that rogue youth leaders are beginning to rise to power. The recent coronation of Ateke Tom, a former militant leader, armed bandit and slaughterer of hundreds of thousands as the Amayanabo of Okochiri, Okrika, Rivers State beggars belief. Before him, the Yoruba nation had also given a highly revered title (Aare Ona Kakanfo) to a man whose thuggish past includes the murdering of thousands of innocent men, women and children extra-judicially. The Igbos are not lagging behind as they produced a separatist leader in the person of Nnamdi Kanu. A man who is a University drop out, an apostle of hate and a 42 year old man still living in his father's house as their Generalissimo-the man they look unto to fight their cause. Can we also forget so soon the overbearing influence of Tompolo, an ex-militant leader, on the Goodluck Jonathan administration as regards appointments and policy making?

Truth be told, in all spheres of our national life, we have young and vibrant people who are giving their best in the pursuit of excellence in their chosen careers of profession. Their numbers may be negligible compared to the whole but they do exist. Even in the political sphere, we have young politicians with ideology and focus willing and able to take over from the old guard.

The government should focus on this excellent crop of individuals especially in the area of appointments if indeed they are desirous of empowering the youths. The media should also celebrate such people so as to encourage other young people to want to follow in their footsteps. The elevation of rogue youth leaders in the society will contribute in no small measure to the further degradation of our value system as it will only encourage many young people to want to make money at all costs seeing that with lots of money in their kitty, they can easily buy respect, honour and influence in the society. I am tempted to believe that this is a deliberate ploy by the old guard to empower their minions so that their interests will be protected when they eventually bow out of power. It is only genuine, selfless and committed youth leaders that can turn out to be true and capable leaders of tomorrow. This is my humble submission.

November 30, 2017.

RETURN OF TOLL GATES

I commend the proposed plan by the Federal Government of Nigeria to reintroduce tollgates on Nigeria's highways. It is quite unfortunate that the plan to reintroduce tollgates which was recently announced by the Honourable Minister of Works, Power and Housing, Mr. Babatunde Fashola rather than attract kudos has received knocks from critical segments of the Nigerian society. Many who should know better have rather chosen to deliberately misinform the public by presenting it as a plan by the government to further increase the hardship of Nigerians in a time of economic recession.

Tolling was initially introduced on Nigerian roads in the 70's in the thick of the oil-boom era. The whole purpose behind it then was that while the money realized from the sale of crude oil internationally would be used to build critical infrastructure like roads, bridges and highways, the money generated from tolling would be used to maintain them. It was not an idea native to Nigeria as it was already in existence in advanced countries of the world like the United Kingdom where we borrowed the idea from and the United States of America.

The whole idea behind the collection of tolls was for road maintenance. However, like all things in Nigeria that got infected by the corruption bug, the money realized from tollgates nationwide began to be diverted into private pockets and that was what prompted former President Olusegun Obasanjo to abolish tolling on our roads and highways in 2003. But despite the corruption involved in revenues derived from the tollgates, it still generated enough funds which was used to still make our roads passable and prevent them from decaying beyond repair. A thorough study of Nigerian roads would reveal that since the abolition of toll gates on our highways, majority of Nigerian roads have metamorphosed into death traps overnight with several avoidable accidents occurring leading to the loss of precious and valuable lives. The huge craters which developed on our roads now became convenient points for dare-devil armed robbers to stage attacks on innocent travellers. It also led to illegal tolling as many motorists in order to avoid bad roads now pass through roads in villages and communities where idle youths now set up their own *"Tollgates"* and collect toll from them.

The way to minimize corruption in the management of tolling revenues is to make it automated. That way, all monies generated would go directly into the coffers of the government. The money realized from tolling should be used strictly for the maintenance of roads and highways in Nigeria and not for any other purpose. That will lead to less accidents on our highways, less armed robbery attacks, less time spent on the road traveling from one place to another and the elimination of illegal tolling on our roads. Alternative routes should be created for motorists who cannot afford to pay toll.

The success of some reputable companies in Nigeria in reintroducing tollgates on some selected roads in Lagos shows that indeed tolling can be successfully carried out in Nigeria. Government should bring in these private companies as consultants in order to pick their brains and get ideas which will ensure the success of this programme all over Nigeria. Our lack of maintenance culture in Nigeria is what has made key infrastructure facilities in Nigeria which we celebrated at their commissioning as world class projects to decay beyond repair and rehabilitation. We must as a people embrace the maintenance culture by embracing the reintroduction of toll gates on our roads and highways.

November 30, 2017.

ATIKU'S ALBATROSS

Alhaji Atiku Abubakar, former Vice President of Nigeria and current Presidential hopeful in the 2019 elections, has been dogged by corruption allegations since the advent of the fourth Republic in Nigeria. Though he has not been convicted of corruption by any court of law both in Nigeria and abroad, he is largely perceived by many Nigerians to be a corrupt politician. Why is this so? Moreso, in a society where perception seems to be greater and more powerful than reality, Atiku has challenged his traducers severally to bring any proof of his alleged corruption while in office but no one seems to have taken up the challenge yet.

Could it be that he has perfectly covered his tracks if indeed it is true that he is corrupt? What about the claim by his critics that he has been banned from traveling to the US because of his corrupt activities? Why has Atiku failed to travel to the US since leaving office as Vice President even when he has a multi-million dollar house in Washington and an American citizen domiciled in the US as one of his wives? Why has he not being prosecuted and charged to court due to the numerous corruption allegations against him since leaving office and losing his immunity from prosecution in 2007?

Atiku Abubakar was the subject of a probe by the US Senate Permanent Subcommittee on Investigations chaired by Senator Carl Levin about 14 years ago. Atiku as Vice President of Nigeria allegedly used some offshore companies-Guernsey Trust Company Nigeria Ltd, Letgo Ltd and Sima Holding Ltd- to transfer about $40 million dollars to more than 30 US bank accounts opened by Mrs. Jennifer Douglas, his fourth wife who is also an American citizen. Also, in a 2008 civil complaint, the US Securities and Exchange Commission alleged that

Mrs. Douglas received over $2 million dollars in bribe payments in 2001 and 2002 from Siemens AG, a major German Corporation. Siemens pleaded guilty to the charges and settled civil charges relating to bribery. Mrs. Douglas, however denied any wrongdoing. In addition, two of the offshore corporations mentioned earlier wire transferred about $14 million dollars over 5 years to American University in Washington to pay for consulting services for American University of Nigeria (AUN), a private University in Nigeria wholly owned by Alhaji Atiku Abubakar.

Closely related to this case was the Jefferson Bribery Scandal. Congressman William Jefferson, who was recently released from prison after spending more than 10 years in jail due to his indictment for fraudulent activities, allegedly paid $500,000 dollars as bribe to then Vice President Atiku Abubakar in order to secure a multi-million dollar contract for his company iGate Incorporated in Nigeria in the year 2003. It was the search for the bribe money that prompted the FBI's raid on Atiku's Washington mansion in 2005. The FBI raid yielded no fruit as no money was found in the house.

All these allegations of corruption, suspicious money transfers and fraternity with corrupt elements in the American society prompted the then US President George W. Bush to issue in 2004 the Presidential Proclamation 7750 denying US visas to foreign officials involved with corruption and Congress later enacted supporting legislation. Those affected by this visa ban include Alhaji Atiku Abubakar, Teodoro Nguema Obiang Mangue, Vice President and son of Teodoro Nguema Obiang Mbasogo, President of Equatorial Guinea and the late Omar Bongo Ondimba, the then President of Gabon among many other foreign leaders.

Here in Nigeria, Mr. Atiku was the subject of investigations by the Economic and Financial Crimes Commission over the misappropriation of $25 million dollars belonging to the Petroleum Technology Development Fund in 2007.

There have also been great speculations by members of the public as to the source of Atiku's great wealth. Before joining politics, Atiku was a Customs officer who rose to the rank of Deputy-Controller General before retiring in 1988. How much is the annual salary of a Customs officer? Yet in just 3 years after his retirement from Customs, Atiku emerged as a multi-billionaire businessman-owning over 150 houses in Yola (his hometown), several farmlands, and unsuccessfully ran for governor in the old Gongola State (Now Taraba and Adamawa) in 1991.

In the book *"Atiku: the story of Atiku Abubakar"*, a biography written by his late friend and who was also his Special Adviser on Media and a veteran journalist, Dr. Adinoyi Onukaba Ojo, we were told the tale of *"Atiku and the miracle of N31,000"*. That Alhaji Atiku secured a loan of N31,000 from a bank in 1971 which he used to build a house in Yola and let it out for rent. The proceeds from the rent on the house was used to build another house which was also let out for rent and so it continued until he became the biggest landlord in Yola and diversified into agriculture.

I do not want to dwell on the veracity or plausibility of this tale but every right thinking adult reading this piece is free to make his/her own deductions and inferences and come to their own conclusions. What baffles me however is the sudden volte face by Atiku last week at a gathering of entrepreneurs in Lagos when he said that he started his business life as a Transporter in 1974 through his ownership of 4 vehicles which he used to transport passengers from Badagry in Nigeria to Porto Novo in Benin Republic while serving as a Customs officer at Idiroko border in Ogun State. This was a story his best friend Dr. Ojo either chose to ignore in his biography or someone decided to invent another tale since the earlier one had been pooh-poohed by critics.

Several prominent Nigerians including former President Olusegun Obasanjo, Kaduna State Governor, Mallam Nasir El-Rufai and former Minister of Defence, General Theophilous Yakubu Danjuma have at one time or the other accused Atiku of corruption. Atiku's spin doctors have a lot of work on their hands as they need to convince Nigerians that all the corruption allegations against their paymasters are untrue, if they desire to see him realize his life-long ambition of ruling Nigeria as President. The last thing that Nigeria desires now is a President who will assume office with corruption allegations hanging over his head like the proverbial Sword of Damocles. It will only lead to a repeat of the Zuma conundrum currently playing out in South Africa. A word is enough for the wise.

December 6, 2017.

RETURN OF SLAVERY

Slavery was abolished internationally over 200 years ago so it came as a rude shock to many when a video filmed and produced by CNN reporter Nima Elbagir surfaced both on CNN and on the New Media showing Africans mostly Nigerians being auctioned off as slaves in Libya. In the video, the auctioneer is seen selling able-bodied men as slaves for $400 dollars. This video which has sparked international outrage with condemnation coming from several quarters has only revealed what has been going on in Libya since the overthrow and killing of the former Libyan Leader, Muammar Gadhafi in 2011.

Though he was no saint, Gadhafi used his power to create a peaceful and prosperous Libya not just for Libyans but for all Africans which prompted many Nigerians nay Africans to settle in Libya and engage in legitimate businesses and pursuits. We also did not hear of slave camps during Gadhafi's long reign in power but those who attempted to migrate illegally to Europe through Libya were sent to prison. Illegal migration is a crime clearly enshrined both in the United Nations statutes and that of almost all the nations in the world, so Gadhafi merely acted in accordance with the law.

He also successfully prevented his people from engaging in atrocious activities against Black Africans due to the well-known hatred and disdain harboured by Arabs against black people. Some have suggested that Gadhafi's love for black people clearly manifested by his almost single handed sponsorship of the Liberation movements in many African countries including South Africa and Zimbabwe, plus his great crush on black women as exemplified by his famous crush on the former American Secretary of State, Miss. Condolezza Rice, was due to the fact that his mother was a black African. But that is neither here nor there as the most important thing was that Africans were protected from the barbarous hordes of Arab tribesmen who see black Africans as less than humans and subject them to dehumanizing and inhuman treatment whenever they encounter one.

That is now history as Arabs tribesmen in Libya, Morocco and Tunisia have returned to their pastime 200 years ago of selling black Africans as slaves. Yes, Morocco and Tunisia are also reportedly involved in this dastardly acts though black Africans do not frequently follow that route to Europe so the atrocities perpetrated against illegal black African migrants there are less reported by the media. Historical evidence suggests that more black Africans were sent to the Arab world as slaves than the New World over 200 years ago. Many of them did not make it alive to the Arab world. They were simply thrown into the sea as food for fish, sharks and other aquatic animals. It is clear that the hatred of the black man by the Arabs did not start today and what is currently going on in Libya is only a reenactment of what their ancestors did over two centuries ago.

There is really no clear cut solution to the human tragedy currently unfolding before our eyes in Libya. But I will say two things. One, that the European Union and Italy place more pressure on the Libyan Transitional Council to stop this modern-day slavery of illegal migrants to Europe. This can be easily done as the EU currently gives annual aid worth millions of euros to the Libyan Coast Guard-the body responsible for intercepting illegal migrants on the high sea and sending them to detention centres. Two, all countries and international organizations who have condemned the human bazaar currently ongoing in Libya and made promises to that effect should put words into action. They should transcend the realm of rhetoric into the realm of activities.

December 6, 2017.

TOWARDS A BENEFICIAL MINIMUM WAGE

It came as a relief to many workers last week when the news emerged of the constitution of a 30-man committee by President Muhammadu Buhari to work out the terms and conditions for an upward review of the minimum wage of workers in the country. It came as no surprise to me considering that President Buhari has consistently shown his love for workers by not retrenching workers during the peak of the economic recession, by paying workers' salaries and allowances as at when due even when there was paucity of funds in the federal purse due to extremely low oil prices at his assumption of office in 2015, by his employment of more workers into the civil service in 2016 and finally by his release of several bailout funds and Paris Club Refunds to enable states fulfill their legal obligations to workers.

That most of the state governors have taken the generosity of the President for granted and hence proceeded to use such funds for other purposes other than that for which it was meant speaks volumes of the caliber of leaders that we have in Nigeria today. While the Nigerian Labour Congress (NLC) and other labour centres in Nigeria have proposed varying figures on what the new minimum wage should be, I am more concerned that the technical committee and President Buhari should rather focus more attention on what needs to be done to ensure that no matter the figures they arrive at, it will be a beneficial minimum wage for workers in Nigeria. Failure to do this will result in a Pyrrhic victory for workers as inflation would inevitably eat up whatever gains they might have intended for workers in the new minimum wage.

One, we need to begin to look at price controls in Nigeria. Once the market sellers, businessmen, landlords, transporters e.t.c hear of an increase in the minimum wage, they immediately jerk up the prices of their goods and services even when there is no corresponding increase in their cost of production. We have seen this scenario happen over and over again anytime there is an increase in the minimum wage in Nigeria. Government should bring back the Price Control Boards which incidentally was very popular and effective during the first incarnation of General Buhari in the 80's with the National Assembly passing legislation to back it up. This will also ensure that the prices of foodstuffs and other essential items do not skyrocket beyond the reach of the ordinary man with the announcement of the new minimum wage.

Two, we need to strengthen our currency viz-a-viz the dollar. It is an open secret that we are running a largely import-dependent economy and most of our businessmen and industrialists spend scarce foreign exchange to purchase raw materials from overseas and then pass on the costs to the consumer. This is the reason why the hardship of Nigerians was severely compounded with the devaluation of our currency in the middle of the economic recession. I am not an economist so I cannot propose any formulas but the economic gurus in the Central Bank of Nigeria and the Ministry of Finance know what to do if the government is truly desirous of strengthening our currency against the dollar.

Finally, the current drop in the prices of foodstuffs nationwide came about because of the campaign by the federal and state governments in the last two years for citizens to embrace agriculture and with the attachment of several incentives to that promise. That campaign should not only be sustained but the government should begin to look at how we can begin to export our surplus agricultural produce in order to earn foreign exchange for the country and boost our foreign reserves. It will also lead to the much talked about diversification of the country's economy and reduce unemployment in the country as agriculture and its allied industries are known to be large employers of labour.

December 7, 2017.

POLITICAL COMEDIES

Wonders they say shall never cease. Nigerian politics, ever full of vagaries and drama lived up to expectations as usual last week. Two governors, Governor Ben Ayade of Cross River State and Governor Rochas Okorocha of Imo State were the major dramatis personae who entertained Nigerians so wonderfully well that not only would the drama be the talk of the town for years to come, generations unborn would definitely make reference to it as one of the most interesting chapters in our journey towards political maturity in our democracy.

Governor Ben Ayade made history as the first Governor in Nigeria to present a N1trillion naira budget (2018 budget) to a State House of Assembly. Before now, the 2017 budget of the state was a whopping N300 billion Naira. Simply defined, a budget is a statement outlining proposed income and expenditure of a country, institution or organization within a time frame. A budget ought to be realistic and based on realistic expectations in order to ensure that it is implemented 100% and satisfies the yearnings and aspirations of the citizenry.

Pray, how does Governor Ayade intend to fund the 2018 N1 Trillion naira budget considering that Cross River State is only an oil producing state on paper having lost most of their oil wells to neighbouring Akwa Ibom State? That is why I find governor Ayade's N1 trillion naira budget not only unrealistic but also a comic relief from the stress of everyday life in Nigeria. Governor Ayade should tell Nigerians the percentage of this year's N300 billion naira budget that was successfully implemented.

The governor's lame defense that much of the money to fund the budget would be realized from foreign investments which will be attracted to the state in the course of the budget implementation does not hold water. This is tantamount to building something on nothing. A man who has never owned a car in his entire life would be considered insane if he suddenly begins to strategize on how to own a private jet.

Stranger than fiction was Governor Okorocha's appointment of his sister as the Commissioner for Happiness and Purpose Fulfillment. While most people have overlooked the lesser *"sin"* which governor Okorocha committed by appointing his sister as a Commissioner which is a gross violation of Nigeria's anti-nepotism laws, the greater *"sin"* which is the appointment of his sister into a phantom office with no clear cut defined aims, objectives and duties, is what Nigerians seem not to be able to overlook. Even illiterate Nigerians know that happiness and purpose fulfillment are individual pursuits and achievements which cannot be determined by or given to the people by any government in the world.

That is why even in prosperous countries of the world, you still find high suicide rates due to lack of happiness and purpose fulfillment while in most third world countries, you will find genuinely happy people content with their meager resources. So what Okorocha has done effectively is to send his sister in search of a godour-in search of nothing. The defense given by the new Commissioner that you also have Ministers with such appellations in some Arab countries can be easily rebutted from two angles. One, such appointments are only done in fascist or totalitarian regimes where the government controls every aspect of the citizens lives.

The Arab countries that were cited as examples are absolute monarchies. Two, the Arab states in question are not only richer than Nigeria but also have very small populations so they can easily afford to splurge money on inanities, luxuries and extravagance in a bid to achieve happiness and purpose fulfillment for their citizens. It is nothing but a classic case of having more money than sense of how to spend it.

If Governor Okorocha is truly desirous of increasing the level of happiness and purpose fulfillment in Imo State, let him pay the complete salaries, allowances and arrears of civil servants, pensioners, contractors, e.t.c

December 11, 2017.

ON THE ANTI-SARS CAMPAIGN

The recent #ENDSARSNOW campaign which has been trending on social media was triggered by an online video showing the aftermath of an alleged killing of an alleged *"yahoo boy"* (Internet fraudster) by men of the Special Anti-Robbery Squad in the Yaba area of Lagos State. This led to a petition that was submitted to the National Assembly last week calling for the scrapping of SARS by Mr. Segun Awosanya which was signed by over 10,000 people. The social media campaign and the submission of the petition against SARS elicited reactions from the police authorities with the Inspector General of Police, Mr. Ibrahim Idris announcing the immediate restructuring of SARS.

The restructuring of SARS as announced by the IGP includes, the *"federalization"* of SARS with a Commissioner of Police in the Force Headquarters becoming the overall head of SARS under the Department of Operations, the setting up of an X-Squad mandated to investigate compliance and abuse by SARS outfits, SARS members will now undergo training in police duties and human rights, and the release of police mobile hotlines for members of the public to lodge complaints whenever necessary.

All these measures by the police have however failed to assuage the feelings of Nigerians as millions of Nigerians have pressed on with the #ENDSARSNOW campaign on social media with rallies billed to hold in major Nigerian cities this week while describing the measures by the police authorities as tokenistic and vowing not to stop until SARS was totally scrapped.

According to the Police Act, the Federal Criminal Investigation and Intelligence Department is the highest investigating arm of the Nigerian Police. This department is divided into 14 sections of which

SARS is one of them. Some of the allegations against SARS include abuse, forceful confiscation of identity cards, women stripped naked and accused of being prostitutes, men were forced to give up their phones and laptops after being accused of involvement in internet scams-and policemen forcing them to ATM's to withdraw thousands of naira as *"settlement fee"*.

This is not the first time in our history that Nigerians have complained about the ineffectiveness of human rights abuses by SARS. We experienced a similar situation in Lagos in the 90's which prompted the formation of Operation Sweep-a security outfit of about 4,000 officers drawn from the Police, Army, Navy and Air-Force, during the tenure of Colonel Mohammed Buba Marwa as Military Administrator of Lagos. However, it did not lead to the scrapping of SARS. It is unfortunate that politicians who should know better have also joined the bandwagon of those calling for the abolition of SARS.

Some like the Rivers State Governor, Chief Nyesom Wike have gone ahead to make outlandish and unsubstantiated claims by saying SARS will be used by the APC-led federal government to rig the 2019 elections. I commend the proposals put forward by the IGP, Mr. Ibrahim Idris, for the restructuring of SARS. He should take it a step further by studying the strategies and tactics used in Operation Sweep so as to learn how to fight criminality with effectiveness, minimal casualties and less abuses of human rights.

Those who say that SARS is biased against the youths easily forget that we have a high rate of criminality among the youths especially in the area of internet fraud popularly called yahoo or yahoo plus. Also, in the event that SARS is abolished, is that not tantamount to giving free reign to armed robbers and criminals of all sorts to freely operate in the society? What is the alternative to SARS considering the fact that a huge chunk of our policemen are currently engaged in VIP protection duty? Are we going to replace SARS with ethnic militias and vigilantes who are not only poorly trained but also engage in extra-judicial killings? We cannot afford to throw away the baby with the bath water just because of the excesses of a few SARS Operatives and Commanders. Restructuring of SARS is the way to go.

December 11, 2017.

CHALLENGES OF NIGERIAN YOUTHS

Once upon a time in Nigeria, we had a Head of State who was 32 years old in the person of General Yakubu Gowon. Chinua Achebe was 27 years old when he wrote the international best-seller, *"Things Fall Apart"*. Peter Enahoro was 23 years old when he became the Editor of a major national newspaper- The Daily Times. Colonel Chukwuemeka Odumegwu Ojukwu, Head of State of the defunct Republic of Biafra, appeared on the cover of the internationally acclaimed Time magazine in 1968 at the age of 33. More recently, Tayo Aderinokun, Segun Agbaje, Femi Pedro, Fola Adeola and others were all less than 30 years of age when they founded Guaranty Trust Bank in the early 90's.

Today, apart from the entertainment industry, you can hardly find any Nigerian youth achieving giant strides in any sector of the society. Despite an avalanche of Youth Empowerment Seminars organized by civil society groups, faith based organizations and non-governmental organizations, the plight of the youths seems to be getting worse by the day. Many graduates of the over 150 tertiary institutions in Nigeria cannot write a 500-word essay on the history of Nigeria, some will tell you that Jamaica is an African country and worse still, a few would tell you that Nigeria's first President is Chief Olusegun Obasanjo.

A famous American politician once said that *"The youths are the trustees of posterity"*. What can the youth do to realize their manifest destiny as the *"Leaders of Tomorrow"*? - apologies to General Olusegun Obasanjo. A cursory study of Nigerian youths today would reveal that their major problem is cowardice. This seeming lack of courage which often manifests itself in many forms is induced by a multiplicity of factors, some of which I will examine in this piece.

Nigerian youths are currently engaged in the pursuit of vanity. By vanity, I mean things which have no impact on your future or destiny but which make you look good today. The overriding ambition of most youths today is the acquisition of material things either legally or illegally with total disregard for the concept of delayed gratification. The embrace of the herd mentality which is a revelation of the lack of courage to stand out from the crowd has only helped catalyze this pursuit of vanity.

The embrace of religion rather than spirituality has also served to keep the youths down in Nigeria. Religion has made many youths abandon logic and reasoning in place of superstitious beliefs and miraculous interventions. It has made many youths to spend hundreds of hours monthly in prayer vigils and church services seeking a miraculous intervention instead of spending those same number of hours at work, studying or developing their talents and abilities which will enable them contribute meaningfully and productively to the Nigerian economy. It has led to the hero-worshipping of so-called men of God.

Men who twist the word of God in order to make gain and who collect money from corrupt politicians while telling their members to accept rigged elections and unpopular government policies as the will of God. Closely related to this is the acceptance of the wrong aspects of African culture and tradition. The dictum that *"It is wrong for a youth to question an elder"* has only served to perpetuate the bondage of the youths. The youth who cannot question wrong practices in the church because of the fear of the anointing and the age of Daddy G.O or Papa will also not be able to lead a protest against the unpopular policies of a 74 year old President popularly called Sai Baba because of the fear of political power and his age.

This has bred docility in humongous proportions in majority of our youths as regards political affairs, a fact that old-school politicians have rightly interpreted as lack of patriotism, lack of courage and excessive love of self. By the way, who wants to give power to people with such demeaning qualities?

The singular most important factor militating against the rise of Nigerian youths in the society is their lack of a reading culture. Most of

Nigeria's young population prefers to spend their money on vanities and inanities; clothes, phones, shoes, parties, cars e.t.c instead of building their intellect which has the capacity to deliver everlasting prosperity to them. How can a young man be dreaming of becoming the governor of a state when he doesn't know the name of the first governor of that state?

The way forward for Nigerian youths is to quit the blame game and embrace entrepreneurship. By entrepreneurship, I do not necessarily imply the creation and ownership of business enterprises though that is also a part of it; rather, I am talking about the employment of their divine deposits, gifts, talents and abilities in order to make a living rather than total dependence on the government for the creation of white-collar or blue-collar jobs as the case may be. This will also imbue them with positive virtues like faith, hope, courage, creativity e.t.c and eliminate the fear of the unknown since they now know that their destiny is in nobody's hands but theirs.

Our youths should endeavour to abandon religion for spirituality. Instead of a rigid adherence to denominationalism and church dogma, they should embrace logic and reason while also adding to its positive spiritual values like truth, honesty, integrity, hard work, thrift, excellence e.t.c as they go about their day-to-day activities and in their worship of God.

Finally, let the youths embrace the reading culture. A popular adage says *"Readers are Leaders"*. We can also turn it the other way round by saying *"Leaders are Readers"*. The bottom line is that if you want to lead then you must read. Reading avails you the opportunity of knowing your rights, duties and obligations as a citizen. It also infuses courage into you to challenge the status quo. Ignorance is an enemy of progress. Our youths must go beyond ranting on social media about unpopular government policies, to writing opinion articles in national dailies, writing open letters to political office holders, writing to their representatives in the national and state houses of assemblies and writing to any ministry, department or agency of government that fails to do its duties in accordance with the law of the land.

They should also learn how to engage in peaceful protests against unpopular government policies no matter how small their numbers may be. Let them join political parties and become active in the political process by standing for elective positions both within the party and for public positions. They should also register and come out to vote on election day instead of sitting at home watching MTV Base on cable television. Power is not given to anybody free of charge rather it is taken by non-violent force. Pardon my use of oxymoron. Let the youths rise and fulfill their manifest destiny. Nigeria awaits your rising.

December 11, 2017.

PDP MISSED IT AGAIN

Since its loss in the 2015 Presidential Elections, the Peoples' Democratic Party, Nigeria's former ruling party cum opposition party has been in tatters. There have been leadership squabbles, unnecessary bickering, rivalry, name-calling and a protracted legal tussle to determine the leadership of the party which climaxed at the Supreme Court. Nigerians expected the PDP to put all their troubles behind them as they headed to the polls to elect new officers at their national convention last week.

They were expected to elect leaders who will enable the party play it's role effectively as the number one opposition party in Nigeria so as to put the APC on its toes and to provide credible alternative policies, advice and suggestions where necessary to the government of the day. But alas! Nigerians only got more of the same with the election of Prince Uche Secondus and other principal officers of the party trailed by allegations of massive vote-buying and imposition and exclusion of certain candidates with aggrieved members walking out of the convention ground angrily and making disparaging statements to the press about the whole process.

The PDP got its political calculus wrong as they have succeeded in alienating the South-West caucus of the party with the non-election of Professor Tunde Adeniran who emerged as their consensus candidate after all the candidates from that region stepped down for him. The South-West is the only region of the party that has not produced a national chairman of the PDP since it was founded in 1998. They also claim that there was a gentleman's agreement within the various caucuses in the PDP to cede the position of National Chairman of the party to the South West- an agreement which accounted for the high number of contestants from that region.

This is a crack in the wall of the PDP which might be easily taken advantage of by the APC in the 2019 elections as the National Leader of the APC, Asiwaju Bola Ahmed Tinubu is not only a skilled strategist and political tactician but is known to have profited from similar political crisis in the Lagos State PDP in times past.

Another significant thing which has emerged from the convention is that the PDP is yet to change from its old ways. There was massive flow of cash in hard currencies on the convention ground ostensibly to buy up the votes of delegates. Also, the circulation of an alleged *"Unity List"* which all delegates were mandated to vote for only shows that the whole process was stage-managed and the PDP is yet to desist from it's a hobby of imposition of candidates during elections. Even the new National Chairman that was elected on Saturday, Prince Uche Secondus, has a lot of corruption baggage on him and might not be able to withstand a thorough scrutiny by the anti-corruption agencies in Nigeria.

Buhari might be perceived by many as an average performer in office but what he has going for him is his integrity or maybe I should say his perceived integrity coupled with his anti-corruption war however selective some may claim that it has been. If the PDP is truly desirous of unseating the APC in 2019, then they should begin to look at presenting credible candidates with little or no corruption baggage on them which they have in abundance.

Just imagine a PDP ticket consisting of Mallam Nuhu Ribadu (President), Chief Okwesiliizie Nwodo (Vice President), Mr. Donald Duke (Director-General of the Campaign Office), Professor Tunde Adeniran (National Chairman) with prominent roles being played in the party by the likes of Mr. Jimi Agbaje, Mr. Peter Obi, Dr. Obiageli Ezekwesili, Dr. Ngozi Okonjo-Iweala e.t.c. That will be a star-studded alliance that is sure of routing the APC from power in 2019. But unfortunately, that will not happen as old habits die hard and if we are to go by the names of those who have currently declared their intention to contest for the office of President under the platform of the PDP. I guess it will be Sai Baba all the way till 2023.

December 15, 2017.

FUNDING THE INSURGENCY WAR

The announcement last week by the Edo State Governor, Mr. Godwin Obaseki, after the meeting of the National Executive Council (NEC) whose members are drawn from Nigeria's 36 state governors and is chaired by the Vice President, Professor Yemi Osinbajo, that Nigerian governors have agreed in principle to approve the withdrawal of $1 billion dollars from the Excess Crude Account have elicited mixed reactions from Nigerians.

The money is meant for the funding of the Nigerian military operations in the North East against the dreaded Boko Haram sect which has waged an 8 year insurgency war against the Nigerian state. The plan by the governors which is yet to be approved has drawn knocks from the Ekiti State Governor, Mr. Ayodele Fayose, and the opposition Peoples Democratic Party with both of them going ahead to make wild claims that the All Progressives Congress led Federal government intends to use the money to rig the 2019 elections in its favour.

It is tragic that Nigeria is arguably one of the few countries in the world where we play politics with everything including security matters. Despite the fierce criticism of and strong opposition to many of his policies, American President Donald Trump was given an $8 billion dollars increase in his military budget proposals for 2017 from $692 billion dollars which he proposed in the budget to $700 billion dollars with approval coming from both sides of the aisles in Congress. Ironically, this budget approval and increase, the highest in 8 years, was given to a President whose foreign policies are geared more towards isolationism than internationalism.

That is why I am stupefied by the attempt by Governor Fayose and the PDP to politicize the attempt to increase military spending at a time when the media is awash with news reports of the resurgence of the Boko Haram sect with attacks on several villages and towns in Borno State in recent times. The resurgence in Boko Haram attacks in Nigeria especially when it is known to have abated significantly since the inception of the Muhammadu Buhari administration which made the Minister of Information, Alhaji Lai Mohammed, to declare that it had been technically defeated in 2016 could be due to a multiplicity of factors. One of them is the collapse of the ISIS Caliphate in Iraq and Syria.

Do not forget that Boko Haram has pledged loyalty to ISIS and even changed its official nomenclature to ISIS West Africa, so it is possible that defeated ISIS fighters and Commanders in the Middle East have relocated to West Africa with their money, and armaments: first, as a safe haven and second to give support to their demented comrades in West Africa.

President Muhammadu Buhari has spent far less money on fighting Boko Haram than his immediate predecessor, Former President Goodluck Jonathan. According to Premium Times, an online news medium, famed for its investigative style of reporting news stories, in a news report on the 25th of September, 2014 claimed that the Goodluck Jonathan administration had spent N1trillion naira ($6 billion dollars at N160=$1dollar exchange rate then) on fighting Boko Haram.

This is besides the $1 billion dollars loan to fight Boko Haram which it secured approval from the Nigerian Senate in 2014, the alleged N2.2 billion naira given to Pastors and Imams for prayers against Boko Haram and the famous $2.1 billion dollars *"Dasukigate"* which was distributed to the top echelons of the PDP and their associates in order to facilitate Dr. Jonathan's re-election in 2015.

All these figures amount to a total of $9.1 billion dollars and N2.2 billion naira and this is not even inclusive of the annual Defence budget during Dr. Jonathan's five years in power. Are you therefore surprised that many serving and retired military officers are currently on trial by the Economic and Financial Crimes Commission (EFCC) for fraud running into several billions of dollars?

This money was originally meant for the purchase of arms and ammunition for the military in the fight against Boko Haram. Buhari's budget spending on Defence (for 2 years) including the proposed $1billion dollars to fight Boko Haram does not in any way come close to Dr. Jonathan's $9.1 billion dollars (exclusive of his annual Defence Budget for 5 years) as it is an open secret that Buhari came to power in a time of economic recession with record-low oil prices internationally, depleted foreign reserves, and an almost empty treasury including a very low balance in the Excess Crude Account so there is no way he could have spent more than Jonathan who ruled in a time of great economic prosperity with oil prices at a record high of $140 billion dollars a barrel.

The fears by some that the $1billion dollars would be embezzled by senior military officers again is unfounded as President Buhari has set up institutional mechanisms to combat this ugly trend which began in the Jonathan era. The recent sack and replacement of some military commanders and soldiers in the theatre of war in the North East bears eloquent testimony of Buhari's resolve to rid the military of corrupt elements.

The military solution to the Boko Haram insurgency which Buhari and the military are pursuing is brilliant and deserves commendation. The long-term plan is to corral civilians inside fortified garrison towns-effectively ceding the countryside to the haramists. The Nigerian military does not have the number and the logistics to effectively police the entire North East due to its large size, sweltering heat and unfavourable weather conditions, and numerous deserts which serve as entry and exit pathways for the haramists to Nigeria from neighbouring countries. Sambisa Forest alone is 5,000 square kilometers which makes it bigger than the whole of Lagos State which is 3,000 square kilometers. Yet, this is just a forest and not even a town in Borno State!

I leave it to you to imagine the sizes of the towns and villages in Borno and the entire North East.

Finally, no amount of money is too much to spend in securing the lives and properties of the citizenry which is the primary purpose of government. Money cannot buy life but it can prevent the loss of lives. I urge all Nigerians to join hands with President Muhammadu Buhari and the military in defeating Boko Haram technically, militarily and pursuing these forces of evil to the gates of hell.

December 18, 2017.

BUHARI @ 75

President Muhammadu Buhari means different things to different people. To some he is a religious bigot and an ethnic chauvinist while others view him as an incorruptible, incorrigible and sincere leader who means well for the country. No matter what side of the divide you stand on, Nigerians should remember that while opinions are free and they are entitled to hold whatever opinion they like about the President, the facts about Buhari are sacred and as such are not subject to debate.

Buhari joined the Nigerian Army in 1961, fought in the Nigerian civil war (1967-1970) and held various positions in the army and in politics before he eventually emerged as Nigeria's Military Head of State in 1983. He was at one time or the other Governor of the North Eastern State, Governor of Borno State and Federal Commissioner for Petroleum and Natural Resources among many other positions.

During Buhari's tenure as Petroleum Minister, the government invested in pipelines and petroleum storage infrastructure. The government built about 21 petroleum storage depots all over the country from Lagos to Maiduguri and from Calabar to Gusau. He also constructed a pipeline network that connected Bonny Terminal and the Port Harcourt Refinery to the depots. In addition to that, he signed a contract for the construction of a refinery in Kaduna and an oil pipeline that will connect the Escravos Oil Terminal to Warri Refinery and the then proposed Kaduna Refinery.

In 1983, when Chadian forces invaded Nigeria in Borno State, Buhari led the military forces that chased them out of the country and even went as far as crossing into Chadian territory in spite of an order given by President Shehu Shagari to withdraw.

As Nigeria's military Head of State from 1983 to 1985, Buhari jailed about 500 corrupt politicians, officials and businessmen for corruption, bribery and embezzlement of state funds. He launched the War Against Indiscipline (WAI) to address the perceived lack of public morality and civic responsibility in the Nigerian society. One of the derivatives of WAI was the law which clearly states that any student over the age of 17 caught cheating in an exam would get 21 years in prison.

After his overthrow in a palace coup led by his Chief of Army Staff, General Ibrahim Badamasi Babangida in 1985, he was jailed in a guarded bungalow in Benin City and was eventually released in 1988. Thereafter, he went into farming and also emerged as the first Chairman of the Katsina Foundation that was founded to encourage social and economic development in Katsina State.

Buhari served as Chairman of the Petroleum Trust Fund (PTF), a body created by the government of General Sani Abacha, and funded from the revenue generated by the increase in prices of petroleum products to pursue developmental projects around the country. A 1998 report in the New African magazine praised the PTF under Buhari for its transparency, calling it *"a rare African success story"*.

Buhari joined politics in 2002 and contested for the Presidency under the platform of the All Nigerian Peoples Party (ANPP) against Former President Olusegun Obasanjo the following year. He went on to contest in the 2007 elections, 2011 elections and 2015 elections against Messrs Umar Musa Yar'adua and Goodluck Jonathan emerging as First Runner-ups in 2007 and 2011and eventually clinching the coveted prize in 2015. Before his death, Nigeria's former Senate President, Dr. Chuba Okadigbo, who was also Buhari's running mate in the 2003 elections, praised Buhari as one of the pillars of democracy in Nigeria and said categorically that Buhari foiled Obasanjo's plan to make Nigeria a one-party state through his entry into Nigerian politics on the side of the opposition.

As Nigeria's President from 2015 till date, Buhari has had an above average performance in office considering the rot and decay in all sectors of the economy which he inherited form the Jonathan administration whose party the PDP had been in power for 16 years. He has laid the foundation for a new Nigeria through investment in critical infrastructure like railways, airports, roads, highways and bridges. Prices of foodstuffs have fallen nationwide due to Buhari's massive investment in agriculture in the last two years. Public electricity supply to households in many parts of Lagos, Ogun and Oyo States have increased to as high as twenty hours a day.

The anti-corruption war has led to the recovery of trillions of naira which has been ploughed back into the economy pulling Nigeria officially out of recession and expanding the economy. Little wonder, that Buhari's N8 trillion naira 2018 budget is the largest ever in the history of Nigeria. He has given two bail-out funds even when he was not obligated to do so and 3 Paris Club Refunds totaling about N1trillion naira to the 36 state governors to enable them offset workers' salaries and arrears due to his love for Nigerian workers.

That the governors have chosen to divert the money for other purposes other than that for which the money was meant cannot be blamed on Buhari but the governors. Buhari promised to focus on 3 major areas if he was elected as President in 2015-economy, security and corruption. It is an indisputable fact that he has performed creditably well in these 3 areas, though he can still do better in the next two years.

As we celebrate the birthday of a great leader, a patriot and a man of destiny, I join millions of Nigerians in wishing the President of the greatest, most populous and most powerful black nation in the world a happy birthday, long life and prosperity.

December 15, 2017.

INNOSON, GTB, EFCC FEUD: MATTERS ARISING

The arrest of Dr. Innocent Chukwuma, founder and CEO of Innoson Motors, in the morning of December 19th, 2017, at his residence in Enugu, by the Economic and Financial Crimes Commission sent shock waves through the Nigerian media space and elicited negative reactions from prominent Nigerians mostly in the South East. It also led to a social media campaign calling on all Igbos to close their accounts with Guaranty Trust Bank, as a form of protest against his arrest, which the bank is widely believed to have been the brains behind it.

While the social media campaign fizzled out without making any significant dent on the finances of GTB and Mr. Chukwuma was released from EFCC detention 48 hours later in Lagos; what I have been unable to understand is the raison d'etre for his arrest as there are 3 different stories making the rounds in the media as the reason for his arrest and they are all emanating from one source - **the EFCC.**

Initial report about the whole saga suggested that the EFCC acted on a complaint against Innoson by GTB over a financial transaction which turned awry. The second report suggests that the EFCC claims that Dr. Chukwuma was arrested for certain tax waivers made in favour of Innoson which it considers fraudulent. The third report claims that Dr. Chukwuma and his brother Charles are being investigated by EFCC over Capital Market and Insurance Fraud to the tune of N1,478,366,000 billion naira. In accordance with the biblical saying *"Whose report do you believe?"* Nigerians are asking the EFCC *"Whose report should we believe?"* Or is Dr. Chukwuma being prosecuted based on all 3 reports?

According to the EFCC, Innoson is accused of stealing motorcycle parts and raw materials belonging to GTB. The motorcycles were ordered by Innoson from its manufacturers and suppliers overseas with a loan from GTB. Under International business rules and because the goods in question were procured with a loan from GTB, the Bills of Ladings and other vital documents needed to clear the goods at the port in Nigeria, were kept in the possession of GTB until the loan was repaid.

The bank accused Innoson of forging banking and shipping documents to clear the goods at the port without its knowledge or approval. Mind you, all of these occurred in the year 2012. Innoson, however denies any wrongdoing in that transaction and according to its spokesperson, Mr. Cornel Osigwe, speaking ex-cathedral *"We have it on good authority that there is a grand conspiracy by an international competitor of Innoson Vehicles who have conspired with a financial institution to pull down Innoson Vehicles at all costs because of the latest increase in patronage of Innoson Vehicles by the federal government"*.

Note, in its defence, Innoson never told us when it paid back the loan said to be worth over a billion naira, how much exactly did it pay back, was it full repayment of partial repayment, and when exactly GTB handed over the documents to them which enabled him to clear the motorcycle parts at the port rather it conceded that its documents were indeed deposited with GTB in the temporary but that permanent ownership lies with it (Innoson). They also did not provide any proof or evidence to back up its claim that there is an international conspiracy against it. Innoson went ahead to make a counter-claim that GTB owes it about N8 billion naira and that the bank told him they could not pay him such a princely sum but rather offered him the bank's shares of the same amount in lieu of cash, an offer Dr. Chukwuma graciously accepted.

The N8 billion naira in question is a judgment debt against GTB for making illegal deductions from Innoson's company account at the Nnewi branch of the bank to the tune of N506 million naira over several years. Innoson went to court and won against GTB but the bone of contention now between Innoson and GTB is the amount of interest to be paid with Innoson arguing that it should be 22% (amounting to N8 billion naira over several years including damages) which is the interest rate that GTB uses in calculating his loan repayments while GTB is insisting that it will calculate the damages based on 7% interest rate.

The issue now is not that of payment of damages to Innoson by GTB but how much to pay since the judgment secured by Innoson from a Federal High Court, Awka, Anambra State did not specify the amount to be paid or the interest rate to be used in calculating the damages to be paid.

The third report that Dr. Chukwuma and his brother Charles are being investigated by the EFCC over Capital Market and Insurance fraud to the tune of N1.4 billion naira is bogus, ambiguous and holds no water since Dr. Chukwuma is not known to have any of his companies quoted on the Nigerian Stock Exchange including Innoson Vehicle Manufacturing. Also, the EFCC did not expatiate, elucidate or give details of the transaction or how the fraud was perpetuated.

The only claim that is uncontested in this saga is the issue of judgment debt against GTB. Why has Innoson waited until this moment instead of seeking a judicial interpretation of the judgment debt awarded him against GTB at the Supreme Court? Even if GTB pays at 7% interest rate, it still amounts to about N2 billion naira so why has GTB not paid or made any attempt to pay rather it resorted to reporting another matter for which it has been defeated in court severally and which is currently pending before the Supreme Court to the EFCC- to do what if i may ask? Also, why would Innoson forge documents to enjoy tax waivers which he is eminently qualified and eligible to get as an industrialist operating in an infant industry in Nigeria and also as an employer of labour?

The EFCC claims that Dr. Chukwuma signed an undertaking to pay his debt to GTB in 2012, yet they couldn't present any evidence of the undertaking that was signed by Dr. Chukwuma 6 years ago not even a photocopy of the original document. Or did the rats eat up the documents shortly after they were allegedly signed at the Enugu office of the EFCC in 2012? Why did GTB, as a law-abiding corporate citizen of Nigeria not go to court with the undertaking allegedly signed by Dr. Chukwuma to enforce the resolutions which he promised to abide by in 2012? Has GTB lost faith in securing justice through the judicial process hence the resort to EFCC- an organization famous for its strong arm tactics and crucifixion of unconvicted individuals in the court of public opinion, for a matter that is currently pending before the Supreme Court?

I condemn in all totality the shabby treatment meted out to Dr. Chukwuma by the EFCC before, during and after his arrest. It should also be clear to all and sundry by now that President Muhammadu Buhari does not hate the Igbos. Federal patronage from the Nigerian military, the Federal Road Safety Corps (FRSC), the Nigerian Immigration Service (NIS) amongst many other federal agencies of government of Innoson vehicles defeats allegations of ethnic bias and witch hunt by the Buhari administration against Igbos.

The way forward is for the President to mandate the EFCC to withdraw from the matter and allow the law to take its course since the case is already at the Supreme Court. All parties should sign an undertaking under the supervision of the Nigerian Police to abide by the judgment of the Supreme Court which is the highest court in the land and put an end to all litigation on this issue. Innoson should also approach the Supreme Court to get a judicial interpretation of the judgment debt awarded him against GTB by the Federal High Court in Awka, Anambra State. The Central Bank of Nigeria should compel GTB to pay the judgment debt against it to Innoson or offer him the bank's shares in lieu of cash.

January 2, 2018.

ON RIVERS KILLINGS

Rivers of blood flowed in Rivers State on New Year's day in Omoku, when over 20 people were killed and 12 more were injured after they were attacked by unknown gunmen as they journeyed home after their participation in New Year's Eve Service in various churches. This blood-letting which was carried out on a day that was meant to be a day of celebration for all has been trailed by condemnation from all and sundry with many calling for the investigation, arrest and prosecution of all those involved in this dastardly act.

It also opened a new chapter in the battle for supremacy in Rivers State politics with the immediate past governor and current Minister of Transportation, Rt. Honourable Rotimi Chibuike Amechi, calling on the governor to resign from office due to his failure to secure lives and properties in the state while the governor, Chief Nyesom Wike, speaking through his Commissioner for Information, Mr. Simeon Okah, accused the former governor of seeking cheap political mileage.

Like most states in Nigeria, Rivers state has always had some history of political violence since the 2003 general elections. Nevertheless, what we are witnessing today is a dimension taken too far especially before, during and after the 2015 general elections. I lived in Rivers state for ten years most of them during the administration of the former governor, Rotimi Amaechi, and i can testify that Rivers state enjoyed relative peace and stability during his reign. Despite *"federal heat"* which was turned on him in the last two years of his administration, there was no upsurge in violence in Rivers state until a few weeks to the 2015 general elections when several APC chieftains were attacked and killed by armed gangs loyal to the PDP.

Notable among those killed are late Chief Christopher Adube and late Mr. Franklin Obi who are both indigenes of Omoku. It was the federal invasion skewed towards the PDP that was responsible for the murderous impunity that turned the 2015 polls in Rivers state into an orgy of violence and slaughter which eventually rendered most of the results of that election nugatory.

The March 19th and December 10th 2016 legislative rerun elections brought an unimaginable harvest of death to Rivers state due to the selfish desire of some politicians to attain power at all costs. In the build up to the elections, there were several beheadings, some were buried alive while others were immolated in various parts of the states. 24 persons were killed in Omoku in one day and in February 2016 alone, 20 people were killed in Ogba/Egbema/Ndoni local government area of the state.

A Deputy Superintendent of Police, Alkali Mohammed was among the notable casualties whose death sparked national outrage. Barrister Ken Astuwete, a lawyer to the former Chairman of Asari-Toru local government area, Chief Ojukaye Flag Amachree, who is an APC chieftain, was murdered in cold-blood by unknown gunmen in 2016. All the political killings in Rivers state have been one-sided so far as there are no recorded killings of any member of the PDP since 2015 till date. It is also a sheer coincidence that Omoku which has been the scene of so much violence and bloodshed in the last two years is the hometown of Chief Felix Obuah a.k.a Go Round who is the chairman of the PDP in Rivers state.

Violence in Rivers state has been provoked mainly by the quest for power. Most politicians in the state see power as the only means of livelihood through access to the commonwealth. It is regrettable but true that in many communities in Rivers state cult gangs hold sway. They control the social and economic souls of the people including the traditional structures which have been rendered impotent. Most of these cult gangs were armed by politicians in the build up to the 2015 general elections. The physical landscape of many communities in Rivers state is painted with boys armed to the teeth and walking about freely to the discomfort of citizens. Loyalty by these criminals to some forces in the Rivers state government has not helped matters.

Governor Nyesom Wike speaking through the then Commissioner for Information, Austin-Tam George, in a report which was published in an online news medium, Premium Times on the 13th of March,2016, blamed the upsurge in violence on a supremacy battle among rival cult gangs in the state. What has he done as the Chief Security Officer of the state to reign in these cult gangs and stem the rising tide of violence? Chief Wike set up a Judicial Commission of Enquiry to probe the violence in the March Legislative Election Rerun, he has allegedly increased funding to the police and other security agencies in the state, he initiated an amnesty programme for all militants, kidnappers and all those engaged in one form of criminal activity or the other in the state, yet all these measures have failed to achieve the desired result.

Wike was a key member of the Amaechi administration as Chief of Staff during Amaechi's first term as governor when in less than a year, Amaechi flushed out all criminals from the state thereby restoring peace and sanity. I therefore find it difficult to believe that he does not know what to do to restore peace in the state. The allegation by his nemesis, Amaechi, that he is fraternizing with all sorts of criminal elements in a bid to win the 2019 gubernatorial election in the state at all cost might turn out to be true. Or how else do you explain the impotence of power in Rivers state to rein in these murderous gangs despite the gargantuan resources, the sophistry of security apparatus coupled with federal support available to the state? Chapter 2, section 14(2b) of the Nigerian constitution states clearly that *"The security and welfare of the people shall be the primary purpose of government"*. Governor Nyesom Wike has not only failed but has obviously run out of ideas on how to fulfill his primary duty of protecting lives and property in Rivers state. I think it is time for him to go.

January 5, 2018.

AN OPEN LETTER TO PRESIDENT MUHAMMADU BUHARI

Your Excellency Sir,

I was born a few years after your reign as Nigeria's military Head of State from December 1983 to August 1985. Growing up as a precocious child with a prodigious talent for reading every and anything in print, I started to read the defunct Concord Newspapers owned by the late business mogul, Chief M.K.O Abiola, at the age of 7 though infrequently. It became more frequent at the age of 10 when my aunt who was living with us at that time secured a job with the Guardian Newspapers so she always brought one free copy home every day which I earnestly devoured with pleasure. Quite naturally, I developed a passion for politics and began to have several discussions with my father about the state of affairs in Nigeria.

One a certain day, while I was lamenting the inability of past Nigerian leaders to make the country great, my father suddenly interjected and uttered the magical words which birthed the feelings that later transmuted into my extreme love for you. Speaking ex-cathedral "The only people who came close to making Nigeria a great country where everything works was the Buhari-Idiagbon regime. They paid back almost all of Nigeria's foreign debt and those of us who were living in Lagos then, came very close to having 24-hours uninterrupted power supply daily.

Though they were poor on human rights, their administration's War Against Indiscipline and Corruption was on course to making Nigeria a corruption-free nation but they were short-lived in power". Instantly, I knew I had found a hero, a mentor and a role model. Someone I could look up to in my quest to see a better Nigeria during my lifetime. I was in Secondary School when you joined politics in 2002 and contested for the 2003 Presidential Elections alongside the colourful, vibrant, and bombastic politician, the late Oyi of Oyi, Dr. Chuba Okadigbo as your running mate. I did not hesitate to give you my support even though I did not have the franchise. I was laughed at, scorned and was the butt of derisive jokes by my family, friends and classmates because of my support for a man many termed *"unelectable"* because of his support for Islamic Fundamentalism.

I was undeterred and continued to support you in the 2007 and 2011 elections with the same cycle of events (with my friends) repeating itself over and over again until mother luck smiled on you in the 2015 elections when you were finally elected as President of the Federal Republic of Nigeria. Mr. President, you promised to do 3 major things for Nigerians if elected into office. They are to fight corruption, rescue the economy from recession and fight insecurity. You have succeeded in the anti-corruption war by recovering trillions of naira of stolen funds.

You have rescued the economy from recession. You have decapitated Boko Haram, recovering territories from the hands of the insurgents. But there is one thing that you lack or have failed to do which not only has the capacity of destroying all your achievements in office or making you lose the 2019 elections but also make posterity pass an unfavourable judgment on your tenure in office as President of Nigeria. This is the issue of insecurity in parts of Nigeria due to the massive loss of lives and destruction of properties by marauding bands of Fulani herdsmen.

I know you are very much aware of the atrocious activities of some of your kinsmen but permit me to cite a few examples, perhaps it might succeed in jolting you out of your inertia on this issue. In Benue State, on New Year Day, over 50 people were sent to the great beyond by Fulani herdsmen who attacked several villages and communities. In 2016, in Agatu local government area of Benue State, Fulani herdsmen killed over 500 in a wave of attacks on villages and communities that lasted several days. An International Agency once wrote in one of its report which was made public that close to 6000 people in Benue State have been killed by Fulani herdsmen between 2011 and 2017.

The South East has also not been spared of the venom of this murderous group. Many villages in Abia, Enugu and Ebonyi have been ransacked by Fulani herdsmen with thousands displaced, women raped, properties looted and many lives lost. Mr. President, permit me to highlight some of the implications of your silence on the menace of Fulani herdsmen in Nigeria. Your silence on this issue gives confirmation to rumours making the rounds that you are a sectional leader who places the interest of your kith and kin above that of the rest of Nigeria. That while you were busy solving the security problems in the core North by fighting Boko Haram, you have deliberately turned a blind eye to issues of insecurity caused by your tribesmen in other parts of the country.

It also reinforces conspiracy theories that you are not in charge of the government. That you are weak, ineffective and indecisive President who has effectively ceded power to a cabal which now superintends over the affairs of Nigeria. Attacks by Fulani herdsmen in the Eastern Nigeria have served to further alienate the Igbos reinforcing several conspiracy theories promoted by secessionist groups like IPOB and MASSOB.

These conspiracy theories include but are not limited to; that you hate Igbos and are hell-bent on punishing them for not voting for you in 2015, that you are out to destroy them at all costs using the Fulani herdsmen and your 97/5 development theory for Nigeria which you allegedly talked about in London is a confirmation of these conspiracy theories. Do you now see the reason why IPOB, MASSOB and other secessionists groups in Eastern Nigeria have cult following alongside several covert and overt sympathizers even among the political class?

Mr. President, your predecessors in office did all that they could to fight insecurity in Nigeria even when such acts were perpetuated by criminal gangs who were from the same tribe with them. Olusegun Obasanjo issued the famous *"shoot-at-sight"* order to security agencies to kill any member of OPC found disturbing the peace in Lagos or any part of Nigeria. Goodluck Ebele Jonathan used federal patronage to silence most of the militant groups in the Niger Delta. The recalcitrant ones among them were silenced by force of arms.

Umar Musa Yar'adua forcefully crushed the Boko Haram rebellion in Maiduguri, Borno State which led to the killing of its leader, Mohammed Yusuf in 2009. Please sir, why is your own case different? I support the call for the immediate proscription of the Miyetti Allah Cattle Breeders Association of Nigeria (MACBAN) and the Miyetti Allah Kautal Hore just the same way IPOB was proscribed by the Nigerian Army and the South East Governors Forum.

It is also an open secret that you were the Grand Patron of MACBAN for several years even up until 2015. Please sir, kindly use your contacts in MACBAN to fish out the criminal elements among them who derive joy from shedding the blood of the innocents and haul them before the temple of justice for immediate prosecution. The security agencies should also be empowered with the latest and up-to-date Intelligence gathering gadgets to forestall future attacks by Fulani herdsmen on innocent citizens.

If you can do all these, it will save me from future shame and embarrassment from family and friends who taunt me daily about the inability of Mr. President to bring an end to the violence perpetuated by his kinsmen against innocent and defenseless civilians. Thank you sir for taking out time to read so long a letter. I still love you.

Your Ardent Supporter

Peter Ovie Akus

January 8, 2018.

THE GENOCIDE IN BENUE MUST STOP

Some people might argue with my use of the term *"genocide"* to describe what is currently going on in Benue, but I think I am justified in doing so. Considering that what is going on in Benue did not start today (it actually started in 2011) and the astronomical figures of deaths that is bandied around in the media (some as high as 10,000 deaths since 2011 till date), I think any rational person should be able to understand my reason for doing so. If you still don't get it, the massacres in Benue are systematic, planned and well-funded by a group of people which i shall talk about later in this piece.

Let me conclude my preamble by giving you some food for thought. How did Ilorin, a predominantly Yoruba town become a Fulani Emirate? How did certain local governments in Plateau State, a predominantly Christian state fall under the control of the Hausa-Fulani who as every historian knows are settlers and not aborigines of the state? Finally, how did black Egypt which produced the pharaohs who built the great pyramids of old become an Arabized Egypt today? Think about these things.

I doubt if President Muhammadu Buhari has the political will to rein in the murderous bands of Fulani herdsmen which are responsible for the genocide in Benue. Since the Usman Dan Fodio led Jihad in the 19th century which overthrew the weak, corrupt, and ineffective kings of the Hausa states, the Fulani Emirs which succeeded them established a new power structure which fused political and religious power in the traditional institution.

That is why the Sultan of Sokoto is the primus inter pares among the Hausa-Fulani Kings in Nigeria; the leader of the Arewa nation and also the leader of over 80 million muslims in Nigeria through his lifetime presidency of the Supreme Council for Islamic Affairs (SCIA). As a matter of fact, for over 30 years after Nigeria's flag independence from Britain, no man could become President, Prime Minister or Military Head of State without the support of the Sultan of Sokoto until General Sani Abacha cut him to size in the mid 90's.

Where am I going with all these stories? Recent revelations in the media have alleged that the trustees of Miyetti Allah Cattle Breeders Association of Nigeria (MACBAN), and the Miyetti Allah Kautal Hore-the apex socio-cultural Fulani organization, includes 5 prominent and powerful traditional rulers in the North who are also Fulanis. Also, there is no prominent Fulani in Nigeria who does not have at least one herd of cattle including President Muhammadu Buhari.

What this implies is that most of the Fulani herdsmen committing these genocidal acts in Benue and elsewhere do not own these cattle but are mere guardians on behalf of their masters who can be found among the top echelons of the society. Therefore any move by Buhari against the Fulani herdsmen or their sponsors will lead to the destruction of his political base in Northern Nigeria where he currently enjoys cult following. Is there still any wonder why despite the biting fuel scarcity and other challenges besetting this administration, millions of people still turned out to receive Buhari in Kano and Kaduna States recently?

The President's sending of the police and not the army to stop the killings in Benue smacks of insincerity and double standards. Why send the army into the south east and rivers state to quell insecurity and then send an ill-equipped, underfunded and corruption ridden police force to do the same in Benue? There are even allegations by some that the real mission of the police in Benue is to prevent reprisal attacks on the Fulani community by aggrieved Benue indigenes and not to maintain peace or arrest the murderous Fulani herdsmen as is being widely touted in the media.

Governor Samuel Ortom should stop wailing like a cry baby and begin to act responsibly as the Chief Security Officer of the state. It should also be clear to him by now that his call for the proscription of MACBAN and Miyetti Allah Kautal Hore, as well as the arrest of their leaders is nothing but a pipe dream that would never materialize. He should begin to distance himself from the President politically if he refuses to take solid steps to stop this menace.

This will send a strong message to the President regarding the 2019 elections as the Benue people voted overwhelmingly for Buhari and the APC in the last general elections. Secondly, he should take the media evidence (including the tweets and the voice recordings) of threats issued by leaders of Miyetti Allah Kautal Hore to annihilate the Benue people as revenge for the alleged rustling of 300 cows and file it as evidence in the International Criminal Court, at the Hague in Netherlands, charging them with crimes against humanity and genocide against the Benue people.

Finally, the governor should urgently send a bill to the state house of assembly seeking the creation of a security outfit in the form of a vigilante whose members would be empowered to bear arms. This security outfit which would be made up of locals would work alongside the security agencies to defend communities and villages from villainous attacks from Fulani pastoralists and for intelligence gathering purposes to forestall future attacks on innocent and hapless citizens.

January 12, 2018.

SACKING SPREE IN KOGI

Last year ended on a sad note for civil servants in Kogi State when 1,774 workers, 8 Permanent Secretaries and some Directors were relieved of their duties by the state government on the 29th of December, 2017. The reason for their dismissal according to the state government is that many of them joined the Civil Service with fake certificates while some were disengaged for engaging in fraudulent activities.

This action has been trailed by widespread condemnation from all and sundry both within and outside Kogi State especially after Mr. Alphonsus Ameh, a Director of Administration and Finance in the state's Pension Board and one of those affected by the retrenchment exercise, suffered a cardiac arrest and died 54 hours after receiving his sack letter. Just like they did last year; when another director in the Civil Service committed suicide due to poverty brought about by the inability of the state government to pay salaries for a year, the governor's spin doctors quickly spun a yarn putting the blame for the doctor's death on himself for his alleged participation in fraudulent activities.

Since Yahaya Bello was elected as Kogi State's chief executive in 2015, he has embarked on a sacking spree of Kogi State workers. In 2017, he sacked 135 lecturers of the Kogi State University and refused to reinstate them despite a court order mandating him to do so. Health workers have been on strike for several months now and the governor has threatened to sack any doctor in the state government's employ who joins the strike.

We were forewarned by the Nigerian Labour Congress during the strike action in Kogi State two years ago about the state government's plan to sack over 60% of the workforce but many did not take heed. Now the governor is seemingly bent on achieving this negative goal without considering its impact on the ordinary man in Kogi State. Does the governor not know that the continuation of this sacking spree will only succeed in increasing the poverty level in the state?

How can a man who has not paid worker's salaries for 17 months be sacking workers? Kogi State has a monthly revenue accrual of N8billion naira monthly yet the governor finds it difficult to pay workers' salaries of N4.8 billion naira monthly. In the midst of all these, the Governor and other political appointees in the state who are supposed to be serving the people have enjoyed constant payment of their salaries and often over-bloated allowances.

The activities of governor bello has only confirmed what I have always believed and known to be true that the most important requirement for leadership is character and competence and not age since governor bello at 42 is currently the youngest governor in Nigeria. The governor's building and commissioning of a multi-million naira mansion in Okene his hometown with pomp and pageantry; his gifting of masquerades with cars and several millions of naira, and his great intolerance of political dissent are just a few examples of the gaffes and missteps of the governor at a time when many are dying of hunger in the state.

I salute the courage of Rev. Fr. John Femi Ogunleye in writing an Open Letter to the Governor outlining the hardships faced by the people of the state and calling on him to change his ways. Kogi State deserves better than this.

January 12, 2018.

STILL ON BENUE KILLINGS

Tears of blood flowed freely from blood shot eyes in Makurdi, Benue state capital when 73 dead bodies, victims of New Year day massacre by Fulani herdsmen were given a mass burial by the Benue State government last week. Notable Benue sons and daughters graced the occasion including the Governor, Dr. Samuel Ortom and as expected there was widespread condemnation of the massacre with some like Chief Paul Unongo, second republic politician and leader of the Northern Elders Forum, who is also the spiritual and ancestral leader of the Benue people, issuing a threat to raise an army to defend the Benue people from such senseless killings by marauding herdsmen in the future.

Some of the developments on this issue of the Benue killings are quite troubling and worrisome. The proposed plan by the Federal Government of Nigeria to establish cattle colonies in all states of the federation to prevent open grazing by Fulani herdsmen has drawn flak from several quarters. The sentimental attachment that most Nigerians of all tribes have to land has made many to rightly or wrongly interpret this move as an integral part of Buhari's plan to Islamize Nigeria.

The Movement for the Actualization of the Sovereign State of Biafra (MASSOB) has issued a warning to the federal government and all Igbo politicians not to attempt or support any attempt to establish cattle colonies anywhere in the south east. I have a problem with the word *"colonies"* as not only does it connotes the subjugation of a group of people but it is also reminiscent of the evils of colonialism that Nigeria suffered under Britain. Why is it so difficult for the government to call it cattle ranches which is the universally accepted name? Could this be a subtle confirmation of the alleged plan by Buhari to continue the 19th century jihad of his forebears towards southern Nigeria until they dip the Sword of Islam into the Atlantic Ocean?

Cattle ranching is a private business both in Nigeria and overseas and even President Muhammadu Buhari himself owns a ranch in Katsina. Does it make financial sense for the government to use tax-payers money to empower people who are engaged in a private business which is neither a significant contributor to our GDP nor a staple which Nigerians cannot do without?

The statement by Anthony Sani, National Secretary of the Arewa Consultative Forum (ACF) concerning the Benue killings is regrettable and should be condemned by all and sundry. He said *"The ACF has set up a committee on how best to handle the anti-open grazing law which has been a bone of contention. The constitution of the committee became necessary because it strongly believed the clashes bordered on occupation rather than ethnicity or religion".* He went ahead to blame governors for enacting laws which are not implementable and Fulani herdsmen for not forgiving those who offended them.

To begin with, his statement on the killings attempted to make it look like a quarrel among brothers which it is not. It is a crime committed against the Benue people and in order to prevent a repeat of such killings in the future, the perpetrators of this dastardly act must be fished out and prosecuted. He also referred to the killings as a clash which it also is not. Rather, it was one-sided as heavily armed Fulani herdsmen descended on innocent and helpless farmers whose only offence was carrying out their legitimate business. Finally, he blamed both the governor and the Fulani herdsmen. In response to that, let it be known to all that Governor Ortom was duly elected by the Benue people to serve and protect their interests.

He was not elected by Fulani herdsmen neither is he supposed to protect their interests. I am not even aware of any Fulanis who are indigenes of Benue State. Is it wrong for the governor to make a law which is in the interest of the people who elected him? Can the governor of Kaduna State make a law which is against the interest of the Hausa-Fulani but in the interest of non-indigenes just because of the presence of a sizeable number of non-indigenes who live and work in the state? What does Anthony Sani mean by saying *"laws that are not implementable"* bearing in mind that he is referring to a state governor and not the Senior Prefect of a secondary school?

I condemn the statements attributed to the governors of Nasarawa and Plateau states, Messrs Umaru Tanko Al-makura and Simon Lalong, that they warned Governor Ortom not to implement the anti-open grazing law as it would lead to unnecessary crisis. They easily forget that it was an attempt by Governor Ortom to put an end to the unending massacres of the Benue people by Fulani herdsmen since 2011 that precipitated the anti-open grazing law in the first instance. Moreover, I consider them as nothing but meddlesome interlopers who rather than focus on governance in their states are more interested in the non-passage of a bill that had over 90% of the Benue people supporting it.

The statements of leaders of Miyetti Allah betrays insensitivity and blackmail. What exactly do they mean when they say *"we condemn the killings but oppose the anti-open grazing law in Benue"*? Let me attempt an interpretation. "The killings in Benue are as a result of the anti-open grazing law. Repeal the law and there will be peace.

When news of the killings first broke, the Inspector General of Police, Mr. Ibrahim Idris said it was a communal clash and only 20 people were killed. It later turned out that it was not a communal clash but an invasion by an armed group and 73 people were killed. When Governor Ortom said that Fulani herdsmen had a camp in Tunga, Awe local government area of Nasarawa State from where they launch attacks on farmers in Benue, the IGP responded by saying that there were processes for arrest and that he would send an investigative team to Nasarawa to verify the governor's claims. Till date, nothing has been heard and no action has been taken. I think the IGP and the police need to recuse themselves from this case as they are incapable of addressing the security challenges in Benue.

The solution to the ongoing genocide is for the military to be drafted in to restore peace through the establishment of a military base in Benue. Governor Samuel Ortom and prominent Benue indigenes both at home and abroad should reach out to the International Community in order to stop this pogrom. Media evidence (voice recordings, video recordings tweet, e.t.c) of threats by leaders of Miyetti Allah to annihilate the Benue people should be filed in the prosecutor's office of the International Criminal Court at the Hague, in the Netherlands charging them with crimes against humanity and genocide against the Benue people. They should also write to and meet with the leaders or the representatives of the leaders of the United Nations, European Union and the five permanent members of the UN Security Council namely U.S.A, Britain, China, Russia and France seeking the labelling of Miyetti Allah as a terrorist group including travel bans and asset freezes on their leaders.

It is a sad commentary on the state of affairs in our nation that the value of human life is next to zero. It is so cheap that to some people the lives of cattle has a greater value than human life. We need to regain our humanity.

January 15, 2018.

NIGERIA, NOT A SHITHOLE?

News reports emerged last week that the American President Donald Trump had allegedly called Haiti, El-Salvador and African countries *"shithole countries"* in a meeting with Congressional leaders about immigration policy in the White House. He allegedly went ahead to say he preferred immigrants from Norway and Asia as they help America economically. Mr. Trump has however denied referring to African nations as shithole countries but said that he used tough words to describe them.

This is not the first time that Donald Trump is attacking Nigeria. In 2016, during the race to win the Republican nomination, he had accused Nigerian leaders of looting Nigeria's money and stashing them overseas. Similarly, in June 2017 during a cabinet meeting, he allegedly said that *"once Nigerians step foot in America, they would not want to return back to their huts in Africa".*

To begin with, let us look at the literal dictionary definition of the word *"shithole".* Simply put, a shithole is a place of physical dirt and shabbiness. With the exception of probably Abuja and Calabar, a drive on most Nigerian roads in the major cities would reveal heaps of refuse, stinking to high heavens, lying on the roadsides unattended to alongside nylons of sachet water and other used consumables.

It is no secret that Nigerians do not have a culture of properly disposing dirt and anywhere that seems convenient for them is where they dump their refuse including gutters which most times leads to flooding during the rainy season. Have we forgotten so soon that just a few years ago, most Nigerians derisively referred to Aba, a commercial city in south east Nigeria, as the *"Refuse Capital of Africa"*. Before we begin to break our heads over what Donald Trump thinks or says about us, we should endeavour to ask ourselves a pertinent question.

How do Nigerians perceive Nigeria? It will shock you to know that most Nigerians in their heart of hearts and despite protestations to the contrary believe that Nigeria is a shithole. Majority of Nigerians who are ranting about Trump's statement on social media are either living overseas, have their children living overseas, have dual citizenship, have investments overseas or are seriously praying to travel overseas one day with the hope of never returning to Nigeria again.

Nigerians played the American Diversity Visa Lottery for several years until they exhausted the quota numbers allotted to the country and were subsequently placed on the list of countries ineligible to apply by the US Immigration authorities. Even while it lasted, some smart Alec quickly turned it into a profitable venture by setting up business centres to aid prospective applicants file their application papers. These are the same set of people who flock churches, mosques, prayer houses, shrines e.t.c and engage in all sorts of spiritual gymnastics in order to secure an American Visa.

We view anything foreign as superior to anything local therefore those who have been privileged to travel outside the shores of Nigeria are seen as superior homo-sapiens which makes many of them possess a superiority complex and an entitlement mentality. A source who is a member of the political class once told me that the reason politicians stash their looted funds overseas is not because they want to keep it far away from the anti-graft agencies but because they secretly fear that Nigeria will implode someday and when it eventually happens they can have something to fall back upon.

I believe this to be true because most Asian leaders who have been accused of corruption at one time or the other have most of their stolen money and investments in their home countries. This means that most Nigerian leaders secretly believe that Nigeria is a shithole which also explains why their wives and children practically live overseas while they govern us here in Nigeria. The tales recounted by several Libya returnees on their return to Nigeria has revealed that Nigerians will do any and everything to get out of the country even if it means riding on camels across the desert and using financial resources which could have been used to set up a profitable business back home. What are they running from in Nigeria? And you say Nigeria is not a shithole?

Critics of President Trump's statement have listed the names of several Nigerians who are successful in America including Adebayo Ogunlesi, a billionaire businessman who was a member of President Trump's Economic Advisory Council and Dr. Bennet Omalu, a medical genius renowned for his discovery and treatment of hitherto unknown injuries which players in the NFL suffer from. What they easily forget is that these men were nobodies when they were in Nigeria and their success can be attributed to the fact they were exposed to superior facilities, superior technology and a conducive environment to practice their craft in America.

They have also cited a New York Times report which listed Nigerians as the most educated immigrant group in America. Yet, despite our great love for education in this country, we are still having puerile arguments over which is more important: the life of a cattle or the life of a human being. I know from personal experience that most Nigerians who live overseas are contributors to the negative image that Nigeria has internationally as they not only look down on their home country but also give a false an often exaggerated narrative of some of the challenges that bedevil our nation to their foreign friends which sometimes acts as a disincentive to foreigners either visiting or investing in our country.

Very few Nigerians who live overseas have houses or investments back home, fewer still have a retirement plan to settle in Nigeria apart from the monthly stipends that they send to their loved ones back home. Why can't they behave like the Indians and the Chinese who invest in their home countries while living overseas and usually have no hopes of living forever in a foreign land?

Most Americans are ignorant about Africa and still believe that people in Africa live in huts and on trees. Some ridiculously believe that South Africa is the capital of Africa. I expect Donald Trump as President of America to have known that. Our problem is political correctness which is largely ingrained in the African culture. We know that Nigeria is indeed a shithole but we have a problem with the messenger (Trump) and not the message. After all, prominent Nigerians have used far more derogatory words to describe the country and they were not crucified. Come to think of it, what kind of words does the ordinary Nigerian use to describe their country in their everyday conversations?

Like all issues in Nigeria, the reactions of Nigerians to the Trump statement has been politicized. PDP apologists have praised Trump while APC apologists have vilified him. I hope this will serve as a wake-up call to our leaders to stop the theatrics and begin the urgent task of building and developing our nation.

January 18, 2018.

RECENT HAPPENINGS IN THE NIA

President Muhammadu Buhari's recent appointment of Mr. Ahmed Rufai Abubakar as the replacement for the sacked Director General of the National Intelligence Agency, Ambassador Ayo Oke, has been trailed by condemnation especially from the southwestern part of the country due to its violation of the federal character principle. Oke and David Babachir Lawal, the former secretary to the government of the federation were both investigated by the same panel headed by the Vice President, Professor Yemi Osinbajo, though for different offences. They were both suspended on the same day, found guilty and dismissed on the same day.

Alas! While Lawal was replaced by Boss Mustapha, his cousin from the same state with him (Adamawa state), Oke, a yoruba was replaced with someone from Katsina State. This appointment by Mr. President does not only betray insensitivity to a region of the country that gave him a bountiful harvest of votes in the 2015 elections, without which he could not have been president but has also fuelled rumours that the president is a sectional leader and that the mainstay of this administration is the elevation of the Hausa-Fulani above other tribes in Nigeria. Pray, are there no qualified Yorubas in the Intelligence community to replace Oke?

The appointment of the new DG is also generating some disquiet in the NIA. Many officers in the agency are questioning Mr Abubakar's competence to lead the NIA. Mr. Abubakar joined the NIA from the

Katsina State civil service under the leadership of his cousin, Ambassador Zakari Ibrahim, in the mid 90's but resigned a few years later due to his failure to pass promotion examination twice and to forestall an imminent sack. While in service, Abubakar violated the agency's regulation forbidding operatives from marrying foreigners by marrying a Moroccan. He is also said to be highly resentful to the US and is anti-Semitic.

He was alleged to have been among those who aborted the scheduled side-talk meeting between President Muhammadu Buhari and the Israeli Prime Minister, Benjamin Netanyahu in New York, during the United Nations General Assembly in September, 2017. If we take into cognizance the brand of politics that the American President Donald Trump is currently playing internationally, a fate that has befallen countries like Pakistan and Palestine as regards American aid and threats to cut off aid to several other nations including the United Nations, can we say that it is politically wise at this time to appoint an anti-American diplomat as the head of the NIA?

Before his appointment as DG of NIA, Abubakar was the Senior Special Assistant on International Affairs to the President and also his Arabic and French interpreter. Many have however fingered Mamman Daura, the President's nephew and Mallam Abba Kyari, the President's Chief of Staff, as the brains behind the appointment and accused them of nepotism and influence peddling. If this is true, then that means the Abubakar is a surrogate and would not be able to record any significant achievement in the NIA throughout his tenure as he would be preoccupied with dancing to the tunes of his godfathers who facilitated his appointment.

In a related development, the House of Representatives is investigating the alleged disappearance of $44 million dollars from the vaults of the NIA just 2 days after the appointment of Mr. Abubakar into the office. It is also investigating Mr. Abubakar's nationality and competence for the job. Mr. Abubakar was born and bred (including his early adult life) in Chad. He married a Chadian in a short-lived marriage and many of his relatives still live there. I wonder how a man with dual or multiple citizenship (he has a Moroccan wife) can be made the head of such a sensitive agency in Nigeria. There are also stories making the rounds that the missing $44 million dollars was moved from the vaults of the NIA based on fears that the new helmsman might tamper with it and that the money is currently in the possession of the Office of the National Security Adviser (ONSA). If these stories are true, then that is an indirect indictment on the integrity of the new NIA helmsman.

I urge the House of Representatives to carry out a thorough investigation of all the controversies surrounding the appointment of the new DG of the NIA. Their findings should form the basis of their recommendations to the Senate who would ultimately determine whether to accept or reject this appointment.

January 18, 2018.

CAMEROUN ANGLOPHONE CRISIS

Since October 1st, 2017, when separatists proclaimed Southern Cameroun as an independent state of Ambazonia, peace has fled the shores of the central African country. There have been riots and violent protests which have led to the deaths of hundreds and displacement of thousands with refugees pouring into neighbouring Nigeria in droves as Camerounian government security forces attempts to crack down on the separatists.

Cameroun was divided between the French and the British before independence in 1960 and english speakers account for 20 percent of the population of 23 million. British Cameroun which is now Southern Cameroun was a part of Eastern Nigeria before 1953. However, a scuffle in the then Eastern House of Assembly, coupled with fears of Igbo hegemony made Southern Cameroun pull out of Eastern Nigeria in 1953 to become an autonomous region under British rule from 1954 till 1960. In 1960, Southern Cameroun wanted to declare itself as an independent republic but was opposed by the British at the United Nations because it was not deemed to be an economically viable enclave.

Interestingly, Bakassi Peninsula which is rich not only in oil and gas deposits but also possesses a plethora of other mineral deposits in commercial quantities is currently located in Southern Cameroun. In 1961, a plebiscite was organized under the auspices of the UN and the Southern Cameroun voted to join La Republique du Cameroun

(French Cameroun) rather than join Nigeria which was the alternative option on the ballot.

However, since 1972 when a referendum conducted by Former President Ahmadu Ahidjou abolished federalism and replaced it with a unitary state, Southern Cameroun commonly referred to as Anglophones because they are English speakers and who are mostly resident in the North West and South West region of the country have been protesting against a bias towards their French speaking compatriots. It must be said that until 1972, federalism gave equal power to the regions while acknowledging their culture and history.

Cameroun's adoption of a unitary state removed most of the protections enjoyed by the Anglophones. A classic example is that in the 1961 constitution, the Vice President (which is statutorily an Anglophone) was the second most important person in state protocol. Today, the Prime Minister (which is statutorily Anglophone) is the 4th most important person in state protocol after the President of the Senate and the President of the National Assembly.

Some years ago, I was friendly with a beautiful Camerounian lawyer who is Anglophone and she used to regale me with stories of how Southern Cameroun was often marginalized by La Republique du Cameroun. She once told me of how her father who is also a lawyer once spent 3 days in the bush hiding from the gendarmerie (military police) after he made critical comments on radio against the government for marginalizing the Anglophones. Let it also be known to all that Southern Cameroun has also attempted to throw off the shackles of domination by La Republique du Cameroun through the political process. Cameroun's major opposition party, the Social Democratic Party was formed in the early 90's by John Fru Ndi to fight for and protect the rights of Anglophones in the country.

Some of the grievances of Southern Cameroun include; the prioritization of French over English in the areas of education, conduct of government business, publication of official documents and public notices and that political appointments including intakes into the military and the civil service in the Anglophone region are biased in favour of the francophones.

The current agitation in Cameroun should serve as a lesson to Nigeria and other African countries who prefer to run a unitary state which most often than not promotes tribal or ethnic hegemony in a heterogeneous society. The solution to the current Anglophone crisis is either of the following. A return to the 1961 federal constitution which guarantees the full rights and privileges of the Anglophones. Or Cameroun's recognition of the independence of the state of Ambazonia. Also, to forestall such crisis from occurring in Nigeria with its attendant loss of lives, we need to restructure Nigeria into a true federal state as it was pre-1966.

January 24, 2018.

OBASANJO'S POWERFUL SALVO

Former President of Nigeria, Chief Olusegun Obasanjo is a man that many are obsessed with. Love him or hate him, you cannot ignore him. Doing so could be at your own peril. Ask Shagari, Babangida, Abacha, Yar'adua and Jonathan. Some have ascribed prophetic powers to him as he possesses an uncanny ability to see into the future. Others see him as an extremely lucky man, a cat with nine lives. To his critics, he is a devil who postures as a saint and sees no good in others except himself. Dr. Obasanjo (Ph.D. in Theology) is a man of letters, who is lettered and has a penchant for writing letters to incumbent Presidents.

His latest letter addressed to President Muhammadu Buhari is titled "THE WAY OUT: A CLARION CALL FOR A COALITION FOR NIGERIA MOVEMENT. In 13 pages, he accused the Buhari administration of failure in the area of nepotism, poor understanding of internal politics and buck passing. He also praised Buhari for his fight against corruption and his efforts to stymie the raging insurgency in the North East.

He delivered the final blow by asking the President not to seek reelection in 2019, berating both the PDP and the APC and calling for a Third Force which he said he is prepared to join in order to salvage Nigeria from tottering on the edge of the precipice and place it on the track of progress and development.

The Federal Government of Nigeria through the Minister of Information, Alhaji Lai Mohammed responded by thanking Obasanjo for praising Buhari on the anti-corruption war and on the efforts to crush insurgency but said that Obasanjo's busy schedule had prevented him from being availed of the efforts of the Buhari administration in other sectors of the economy. He went ahead to list several achievements of the Buhari administration since assuming power in 2015.

There have been divergent reactions to Obasanjo's political epistle to President Buhari. Supporters of the President have berated Obasanjo for the letter saying he lacks the moral fibre to lecture Buhari on issues of governance as he is one of those responsible for the rot in Nigeria which Buhari is trying so hard to clear. While supporters of the Former President have praised him for speaking the truth and standing up for the suffering masses labeling him as the conscience of the nation.

I have read and reread the letter many times over and arrived at the conclusion that there is really nothing new in what Obasanjo has said other than the fact that he asked Buhari not to seek reelection in 2019. Many prominent Nigerians overtly and covertly including members of the ruling APC have accused the President of either the same or similar misdemeanors in his approach to statecraft in times past. Even his better half broke ranks with him last year threatening not to campaign for him in 2019. Can you tell me who else will know or understand a man better than his wife who lives, eats, and sleeps with him in the same house?

Elections in any nation are not won based on achievements alone. Usually, there are one or two issues which if not properly managed might lead to the defeat of an incumbent despite his/her stellar performance in office. Goodluck Jonathan lost the Presidential elections in 2015 due to his inability to curtail corruption and crush the Boko Haram insurgency even though he had wonderful achievements in the area of Agriculture, Entertainment, Youth Empowerment, Economy (until 2014), Transportation (Aviation and Railways), Communications e.t.c.

Also, Hillary Clinton lost the 2016 Presidential elections to Donald Trump despite her achievements and long years of public service because that election was not about experience but about the common man in America who was losing jobs to either foreigners overseas or to illegal immigrants in the country and Donald Trump presented himself as the man with the magic wand to reverse that ugly trend. Truth be told, If Buhari fails to handle the issue of the killings by suspected Fulani herdsmen properly and also address some of the critical issues raised by Obasanjo in the letter, he can as well kiss 2019 goodbye.

Take it or leave it, it is an undeniable fact that Obasanjo is a man of destiny. At various times, when Nigeria tottered on the edge of the precipice, he was the instrument used by God to salvage the country. He did it during the civil war as the commander of the famous 3rd Marine Commando who received the Biafran instrument of surrender thus bringing an end to 30 months of fratricidal bloodbath. He has also been the scourge of dictatorial, corrupt, inept, and weak leaders whether military or civilian through his verbal or written missiles advocating for good governance on behalf of the suffering masses of Nigeria.

In office either as President or Military Head of State, he scored an A in foreign affairs and remains till date the most globally recognized Nigerian leader whether dead or alive. I will score him a C in terms of his developmental initiatives for the country, though much of his failures can be attributed to the activities of corrupt party apparatchiks, corrupt bureaucrats and his own personal failings. As regards the Third Force, it should be a grand coalition made up of individuals who mean well for Nigeria and who have not been smeared with the tar of corruption. Members should be drawn from groups such as ideologically driven political parties, student unions, civil society organizations, labour unions, professionals, youth groups e.t.c. They should also endeavour to present candidates with character and competence that would give both the APC and the PDP a run for their money in 2019.

January 29, 2018.

BBOG CAMPAIGNERS' MARCH ON THE VILLA

On the night of 14th April 2014, 276 female students were kidnapped from their dormitories in Government Secondary School, Chibok, Borno State. Boko Haram, a terrorist group which has carried out several attacks in the West African sub-region, claimed responsibility for the kidnappings even as 57 of the girls managed to escape from captivity due to the fact that the vehicles their captors used to ferry them away was overloaded and the brave ones among them jumped into the bush while the vehicle was in motion.

This was the incident that birthed the Bring Back Our Girls Campaign led by Mrs. Oby Ezekwesili, a former Minister of Education, and Mrs. Aisha Yesufu, a social activist. I commend the BBOG campaigners for their single mindedness and their tenacity of purpose despite insults, name calling and intimidation from government security forces, for not allowing the issue to be swept under the carpet as is the norm in Nigeria, and for their partial success evidenced by the return of half of the captured girls.

The fact that they are still involved in the campaign despite a change in government at the federal level has also debunked rumours which made the rounds that they were sponsored by the then opposition All Progressives Congress to bring down the administration of Former President Goodluck Jonathan.

However, I think it is time for the BBOG campaigners to consider a change of strategy in line with the current realities if they are truly desirous of actualizing their aims and objectives. I say this in view of the clash between the Police and the BBOG campaigners when they (BBOG) attempted to march on the Presidential Palace. While i condemn all forms of brutality by the police, if indeed there was any, the BBOG campaigners especially Mrs. Ezekwesili, who has been in government before, should have known that a march on the Presidential Palace is a security risk and it would be a failing on the part of the Police and other security agencies if they failed to stop the marchers.

There is nowhere in the world where protesters are allowed to march onto the grounds of the Presidential Palace. Not even in America, where they have an open, free and liberal democracy. How much more Nigeria which is bedeviled with a plethora of security challenges, left, right and centre? The Police was also wrong to have arrested the protesters since they committed no crime. Those in the administration who ordered the arrest of the BBOG campaigners should not fail to remember that they were the major beneficiaries of the campaign as it is an open secret that the issue of the Chibok girls was the Achilles heel that led to the downfall of the past administration.

They (BBOG) should be patient with the government seeing that the government has secured the release of half of the girls in captivity, has promised to free the remaining 112 girls, and has renewed the fight against their captors. They should also lower the bar of their expectations since recent videos posted on the internet by the insurgents have revealed that some of the girls are now married to their captors with children and have expressed a desire not to return back to their families in Nigeria.

It will be extremely difficult for the security agencies to secure the release of some of them who have been brainwashed into becoming fighters for Boko Haram or those who are currently experiencing Stockholm Syndrome. BBOG campaigners should be mindful of the fact that the recent resurgence of Boko Haram with attacks on several villages and communities, can be attributed to the alleged release of some Boko Haram leaders in prison coupled with a large amount of money (several millions of dollars) in exchange for the released Chibok girls.

BBOG campaigners can camp out, carry out rallies, campaigns, grant interviews and engage in advocacy rather than attempting to march on the Presidential Palace every now and then. They should be less antagonistic towards the government but should collaborate with them as partners in progress in securing the release of the remaining Chibok girls.

January 29, 2018.

NOT OBJ'S THIRD FORCE

It was Professor Wole Soyinka that first introduced the word *"Third Force"* into Nigeria's political lexicon. In 1967, during the Nigerian civil war, Biafran forces led by Brigadier Victor Banjo, a Yoruba, overran the Mid-West and were speedily heading towards Lagos to unseat General Yakubu Gowon and capture Nigeria's federal capital city when they suddenly stopped at Ore, a town in Ondo State. While many wondered about the reason for the sudden stop even when they faced little or no resistance; with General Chukwuemeka Odumegwu Ojukwu, the Biafran leader, barking out orders from Enugu for the mission to proceed immediately to Lagos, an instruction which fell on deaf ears, Professor Soyinka, in his memoirs titled *"You must set forth at dawn"*, reveals the reason for the delay by Banjo which not only changed the course of the war but also altered the course of Nigeria's history.

Apparently, Brigadier Banjo, unwilling to shed Yoruba blood, had sent Soyinka as an emissary to deliver a message to Major Olusegun Obasanjo, who was the commander of Nigeria's military forces in the Western region, to allow easy passage of Biafran troops to Lagos. He also revealed that his true intentions was not to divide Nigeria but to unify the country as part of a Third Force comprising of soldiers both in Nigeria and Biafra, who saw the war as a clash of egos between two men (Ojukwu and Gowon) and proposed a solution to the crises by toppling both regimes, bringing an end to the war, and unifying the country. Obasanjo snitched on Soyinka to the federal authorities who promptly clamped him into detention until the end of the war. While Brigadier Banjo, Major Emmanuel Ifeajuna, and other suspected members of the Third Force in Bafra were recalled to Enugu where they were shot at the stakes after they were court-martialed by the military authorities. The recent call for a Third Force by the same person who frustrated the success of the initial Third Force, is not unconnected with the failure of the 1st Force (PDP) and the 2nd Force (APC), to satisfy the yearnings and aspirations of the Nigerian people. However, here is a caveat, we must not mistake Obasanjo's Coalition for Nigeria Movement as the Third Force that we desire or seek. As a matter of fact, Obasanjo's new group must be avoided like the plague by all well-meaning Nigerians who are truly desirous of changing the supposed change that we are currently experiencing in Nigeria. My reason for saying this is neither far-fetched nor are my fears unfounded. The Coalition for Nigeria Movement is largely made up of political disciples of the former president some of whom were accused of vote rigging in times past and evicted from power by judicial pronouncement from the temple of justice. Others have corruption cases hanging over their heads like the proverbial sword of Damocles. Additionally, most of them are politicians who were once members of the PDP and the APC and that includes Prince Olagunsoye Oyinlola, the former Governor of Osun State who is the Convener of the movement.

We cannot allow spent forces to be members of the proposed Third Force. Also, if we accept CNM as the Third Force, that means we have given Obasanjo another opportunity to produce Nigeria's President again and whosoever emerges as President would be beholden to him and not the Nigerian people. Obasanjo's personal failings are all too obvious so rather than play a direct role in the proposed Third Force, he should rather play an advisory role. What we need is a granite coalition made up of several interest groups and stakeholders in the Nigerian Project. The Nigerian Intervention Movement, the Red Card Movement, CSO's, Labour Unions, Professional bodies and even CNM should coalesce together to form the Third Force. It should transmute from a political movement into a political party that would present credible and competent candidates at all levels of governance in this country in the 2019 elections.

The Third Force will need to act fast as the 2019 elections is just about a year away. The Third Force should be ideologically driven and its major ideological plank should be the restructuring of Nigeria or the devolution of powers from the center to the various federating units. Nigeria is arguably the only federal republic in the world that has about 62 items on its exclusive list. That implies too much workload on the federal government and that is why whenever anything bad happens in any part of Nigeria, we blame it all on the President. For example, if we have state police and even community police, why would anyone blame President Muhammadu Buhari for the killings by supposed Fulani herdsmen in various parts of Nigeria? I dare say that contrary to President Buhari's New Year Day homily to Nigerians, Nigeria's problems are more about structure than processes. There should be an aggressive social media campaign to encourage the youths who constitute about half of Nigeria's population and who mostly bear the brunt of the bad policies of our leaders, to stop the online rant and vent, register to vote, collect their PVC's and come out en masse on election day to vote and protect their votes if need be.

Money is a critical factor in any election and some have blamed the dirty money given by dirty politicians to the ruling APC in the 2015 elections as the reason for the indecisiveness of the President on some critical national issues. Therefore the Third Force would need to generate its campaign funds directly from the people through crowd-funding both online and offline. This would automatically make the Nigerian people the godfathers of the Third Force and all the evils and shenanigans associated with god-fatherism in our political system would be absent in this new political party. In conclusion, Nigerians need to know that the success or failure of the Third Force is directly dependent on them and not the politicians. They must shun the *"siddon look"* mentality and must be actively involved in the political process at least at the level of voting. Nigeria belongs to all and not the politicians alone.

February 2, 2018.

SENATE AND CUSTOMS BOSS FEUD

The last may not have been heard about the crisis between the Nigerian Senate and the Comptroller General of the Nigerian Customs Service, Colonel Hameed Ali (rtd). This time the disagreement was over protocols when Senator Dino Melaye (APC, Kogi West), led other members of the Senate Ad-hoc committee on Economic Waste in the Nigerian Customs Service to visit the national headquarters of the NCS. The recent exchange of words between the Senators and the Customs boss was triggered by remarks made by Melaye during the meeting that the Comptroller General by way of protocol, ought to have come down from his office to welcome and usher the committee members into the premises and not just meeting them at the conference room. He further went ahead to say that was the protocol and practice of bodies like the Customs and Immigration over the years.

The CGC, Colonel Ali replied by saying that the Customs has its own protocol which are quite different from those of other establishments, insisting that the agency would not allow itself to be dictated to on matters of etiquette or protocol adding that *"nobody in the Senate or House of Representatives has ever come out to receive us when we visit".* He also said that it is the committee that is supposed to visit him in the office before they proceed to the conference room.

Irked by the retort of the CGC, members of the Senate Ad-hoc committee refused to take photographs with the top management of the Customs at the end of the meeting as is customary. Their negative reaction to his reply by refusing to take photographs with the top management officials angered Colonel Ali, who stormed out of the conference room into his waiting convoy and drove out of the premises. Allegations were later made by the senators that Colonel Ali used his convoy to prevent the lawmakers from leaving the premises before him. It will be recalled that the Customs boss has had a running battle with the entire Senate between 2016 and early 2017 over his decision to dress in mufti and not uniform. In the first place, the senate committee was obviously on a witch hunt because I do not understand the reason behind the setting up of an ad-hoc committee with a bogus mandate to probe the Customs. How do you define economic waste in a paramilitary agency knowing fully well that such definitions could be subjective and that no member of the committee has a background in the security sector?

For example, if the NCS spent N100 million naira in a particular year on informants who gave information about smuggling routes into the country including the location of warehouses where these contraband are stored, would that also be classified as economic waste? If the senate committee is not on a witch hunt following the altercation it had with the CGC a year ago, then why did they not set up a committee instead to probe economic waste in all the MDA's instead of the Customs alone?

The connotative meaning of the word *"Protocol"* as used by both speakers means an accepted code of behaviour in an organization. We must also note that most times protocol in an organization is usually unwritten. Dino Melaye and other members of the senate committee have never been members of the NCS, so how did they know the protocol of the NCS as they allege? Are the members of the senate ad-hoc committee not also aware that it is against protocol not to take photographs with top management of an organization that you are visiting?

The character of the individual chosen to head the senate ad-hoc committee is also in doubt as not only does he court controversy with his words, deeds and lifestyle but also because he seems to be more adept at waxing hit songs than making laws which he was elected to do. If we are to accept the Senators' obsession with protocol, are they not also aware that it is against the protocol of the Nigerian Army, for a senior officer like Ali, who served meritoriously in an illustrious career spanning decades and retired honourably, to put on the uniform of the paramilitary agency that he currently overseas?

The Customs boss is an achiever who last year alone raked in over a trillion naira into the federal coffers as revenue collected by the NCS- an achievement which is unprecedented in the annals of the organization and the nation. The Nigerian Senate should focus on its primary duty of making laws than playing the role of a meddlesome interloper in the NCS. Colonel Hameed Ali (rtd) should not be obstructed from doing the good work he is currently undertaking in the agency due to the pettiness of our senators.

February 2, 2018.

KENYA: NOT YET UHURU

Not Yet Uhuru is the title of the autobiography written by Jaramogi Oginga Odinga, Kenya's First Vice President, and father of the man in the eyes of the storm, Raila Odinga. Uhuru is a Swahili word which means freedom.

It all started with the August 8th, 2017 elections in which President Uhuru Kenyatta was declared winner for a second term. Odinga challenged the results at the Supreme Court which nullified the results and fixed a re-run for October 26, 2017, an election Odinga boycotted citing a lack of electoral reforms and which Kenyatta won with a landslide.

Last week, in an apparent fulfillment of a threat he issued after the October re-run elections, Odinga was sworn in as the *"People's President"* at Uhuru park, Nairobi, a potentially treasonable act punishable by death under Kenyan law. President Kenyatta responded swiftly by ordering a massive crackdown on media coverage of the event which led to the shuttering of 3 private television stations, followed immediately by a government gazette declaring the National Resistance Movement, NRM, the "C" wing of Odinga's party, the National Super Alliance, NASA, as an "organized criminal group".

Before we begin to apportion blame as to who is right or wrong, between Kenyatta and Odinga, it is proper to establish certain facts regarding the Kenyan elections. In the build up to the August elections, the mutilated body of Chris Msando, acting Director for Information and Communications Technology at the Independent Elections and

Boundaries Commission (IEBC), Kenya's electoral commission, was found in a forest near the capital Nairobi. Also, in the build up to the October re-run elections, Roselyn Akombe, a senior official in the electoral commission, resigned and fled to the United States of America, saying members of the commission were under intense pressure from *"unnamed sources"* to compromise the vote and that she felt her life was no longer safe in Kenya. Both incidents seemingly corroborates Mr. Odinga's claim that the elections were rigged by hackers who infiltrated the database of the election body to manipulate the results, and that members of the IEBC led by Mr. Wafula Chebukati, were biased in favour of the incumbent.

Furthermore, the Supreme Court verdict which annulled the initial elections, clearly stated that the IEBC did not have all the tally forms when they announced the results. It also said that some forms lacked security features such as watermarks, signatures or serial numbers, which called their authenticity into question. It is pertinent to ask why IEBC refused the Supreme Court access to its computer system in order to enable it verify opposition claims of hacking?

We must also not overlook the covert and overt intimidation of the judiciary by President Kenyatta and his allies after the Supreme Court nullified the August poll. The shooting of a bodyguard of a member of Kenya's Supreme Court, Deputy Chief Justice Philomena Mwilu and the utterances of Kenyatta about the Supreme Court Judges after the annulment of the August poll lends credence to my assertion.

The political feud between Kenyatta and Odinga is reminiscent of that which existed between their fathers, Jomo Kenyatta and Jamarogi Oginga Odinga, Kenya's first President and Vice President respectively, one a Liberation war veteran, the other a wealthy supporter of the Liberation war, who fell out with each other politically and became bitter enemies until their deaths. It seems to me that there is a calculated plan by the Kikuyu to monopolize power and perpetuate their hegemony in Kenyan politics. With the exception of Daniel Arap Moi, Kenya's longest serving ruler, who is a Kalenjin, whom Jomo Kenyatta appointed to the Vice Presidency, named as his successor and stubbornly refused to dismiss despite several pleas by his tribesmen urging him to do so, all of Kenya's Presidents have all been Kikuyu.

Many have speculated that Odinga's plan is to foment civil unrest so as to force the government to the negotiating table and make them implement electoral reforms before a fresh election is conducted. That is a feasible plan considering that Odinga has rock star popularity in Kenya especially among the poor and rural dwellers. It also explains why he did not declare himself as the President of Kenya rather he declared himself as the *"People's President"* thus laying the foundation for a long drawn legal challenge, if it arises, with its many twists and turns, to the Presidency of Uhuru Kenyatta.

It is a political booby trap which Kenyatta seems to be falling for with the recent closure of some media houses, the arrests of journalists, lawyers and political associates of Odinga, actions which have attracted widespread condemnation and sparked international outrage. Let us not forget that a similar scenario played out after the 2007 elections won by Former President Mwai Kibaki. Violence trailed the announcement of the results with over a thousand killed and about 600,000 displaced before former United Nations Secretary General, Mr. Kofi Annan negotiated a coalition government in which Kibaki was President while Odinga was Prime Minister.

The battle for the soul of Kenya is on. Political warlords in East Africa's biggest economy should be mindful of the fact that a prolonged crisis could be fatal for the country as it could attract terrorists in prophetic in his autobiography published over 3 decades ago. Indeed, it is not yet Uhuru in Kenya.

February 8, 2018.

MARADONA DOES IT AGAIN

His style of leadership, coupled with the fact that he reigned at a time when the legendary Argentine footballer, Diego Amando Maradona, dazzled the world with his dribbling skills on the field of play, earned him the nickname *"Maradona"*. General Ibrahim Badamasi Babangida, Nigeria's self-styled Former Military Head of State and self-proclaimed *"Evil-Genius"*, is a sly character, gifted with cunning, famous for prevaricating on national issues, skillful at issuing vague and ambiguous statements, and master of doublespeak. e is at it again. This time it is about a press statement issued by his spokesperson, Prince Kassim Afegbua last Sunday, in which he commented on the state of affairs in the nation and allegedly asked President Muhammadu Buhari not to seek a second term in 2019. Hours after the release of the press statement, another press statement allegedly emanating from the gap toothed General was released denouncing the initial press statement issued by Afegbua.

The second press statement did not ask Buhari not to run in 2019 but said that the Former Head of State would explore other channels in communicating his thoughts about the state of affairs in Nigeria to President Muhammadu Buhari. However, in a new twist to the story, IBB spoke to THIS DAY newspaper on Monday, and affirmed that he indeed authorized the initial statement issued by Afegbua, and that the second press statement was issued by his *"friends"* on his behalf. Meanwhile, the Inspector General of Police, Mr. Ibrahim Idris had declared Mr. Afegbua wanted for defamation of character just hours after the release of the second press statement. I have read both press statements and the only difference between them is where IBB allegedly asked Buhari not to seek a second term. I must say though that in the initial press statement issued by Afebua, IBB made a subtle, veiled and indirect call on President Buhari not to contest in 2019, while in the second statement there was nothing of such.

I say so because in comparison to the press statement issued by Former President Olusegun Obasanjo, calling on Buhari not to contest in 2019, IBB's press statement lacked direct, brutally frank, concise, and precise words. He seemed to be making suggestions rather than definitive statements unlike OBJ who employed more of the latter than the former. Arguably, the difference in the choice of words is a reflection of the difference in their personalities.

Here are some posers which might help us resolve this conundrum with Solomonic wisdom. Is it possible for Afegbua to release a press statement on his own without authorization from his principal? Did Babangida make a complaint to the IGP about the altering or the unauthorized release of a press statement in his name by Afegbua?

On whose instruction did the IGP act upon to declare Afegbua wanted? A declaration which is illegal anyway presuming Afegbua was guilty because he was not given up to 24 hours to present himself to the Police authorities before he was declared wanted. More so, this is a civil matter and not a criminal matter so the proper thing to do is to file libel charges against Afegbua in a civil court and that should be the call of IBB not the IGP.

The release of a press statement by General Babangida barely two weeks after Obasanjo's missive to Buhari, both counselling him not to seek reelection in 2019 could be indicative of something fishy. Perhaps, it is reflective of the outcome of the meeting held last year by Generals OBJ, IBB, and Abdulsalami Abubakar at Babangida's hilltop mansion in Minna, Niger State, while Buhari was battling for his life in a London hospital. Meaning, we should be expecting General Abubakar to be next in line to launch a missive at Buhari asking him not to run in 2019. I am really not surprised at this whole brouhaha over IBB's press statement. He has done similar things in times past. I fear Afegbua could be the fall guy in this latest episode.

I think that the time has come for Prince Kassim Afegbua to sever his relationship with a General who has manifested more of cowardice than courage in civil life. A man who cannot deliver himself from the hands of his friends. The same friends who piled pressure on him to annul the June 12, 1993, Presidential Elections, Nigeria's freest and fairest, since independence in 1960 till date. The IGP is a meddlesome interloper in this issue. It is curious that he was quick to act on Afegbua but is lethargic on the issue of killings by Fulani herdsmen. Probably someone in Aso Rock is jittery about 2019.

February 8, 2018.

JANG AND NIGERIAN YOUTHS

Former Governor of Plateau State, and current Senator of the Federal Republic of Nigeria, Mr. David Jonah Jang, goofed when he said on a radio show in his home state, that the *"Nigerian Senate is not meant for young people"*. Coming from the mouth of someone who was privileged to govern two states (Benue and Old Gongola States) as a young man, this statement is borne out of selfishness, malice, hatred and political mischief. I understand that the statement was a veiled reference to his political opponents in the PDP who are desirous of unseating him as a senator in 2019; all the same, it is still a statement in bad taste.

It is pertinent to inform Jang that there is no provision or clause in the Nigerian constitution that precludes young people from being in the Senate. Once a man/woman attains the age of 35, is of sound mind, has never been declared bankrupt, among other statutory requirements which also apply to older Nigerians seeking political office, then he/she is good to go.

The task of governing a state is more arduous and cumbersome than the task of representing a third of a state as a parliamentarian. If Jonah Jang could carry out that task, as Governor of two states, where he is said to have performed creditably well, as a young man, what makes him think that the youths of today cannot carry out the task of law making? It is true that all over the world, the Senate is for mature people who have paid their dues. But it is also true that maturity is not a function of age.

I am of the opinion that leadership is not a function of age but of character and competence. America, the number one democracy in the world, elected a 70 year old man as their President, at a time when most European countries are electing leaders in their 30's into office. Can Jang tell us the contributions of geriatric lawmakers in the Nigerian Senate other than sleeping during plenary?

At the dawn of the Fourth Republic, we had a lot of young men and women who were members of the Nigerian Senate and they performed excellently well in office. Senator Tokunbo Afikuyomi, was the youngest member of the Senate at the age of 37 and one of its best and brightest. Senator Anyim Pius Anyim became a Senator at the age of 38 and became the Senate President at the age of 39, thus making him the youngest occupant of that seat in Nigeria's recent history.

We must also not fail to note that our political system is so polluted that even if all the levers of power in the country are handed over to the youths, they will be polluted by the system and fail to achieve their aims and objectives. The youths need to unite and form a critical mass to change the system both within and without. We must stop supporting and applauding *"old cargoes"* who only view us as expendables to deploy in their quest to attain power. Nigeria belongs to all.

February 12, 2018.

OSINBAJO AND THE CALL FOR STATE POLICE

I support Vice President Yemi Osinbajo's call for the creation of State Police. I hope it is not a ploy by the APC led federal government to hoodwink Nigerians on the issue of Restructuring as we approach 2019. I commend the Nigerian Governors Forum (NGF), for backing the VP's call and proposing modalities on how it can be implemented in the various states of the federation.

The major argument adduced by those who oppose state policing is the immaturity of politicians in our clime, especially the governors, who will be the major beneficiaries, and their proclivity towards abuse of power. The powers of the President to declare a State of Emergency in any state of the federation, where there is a breakdown of law and order, and to appoint an interim administrator in lieu of the governor, will serve as a check against this. Any governor who abuses his powers can be easily voted out by the electorate in the next elections.

The governors would also have it at the back of their mind that they are occupying a tenured office and if they use State Police as an instrument of vendetta against their opponents while in power, similar measures might be meted to them by their successors when they are out of power. The argument that they will be used to rig elections in favour of incumbents does not hold water as politicians in different political parties have also used the current Federal Police to rig out their opponents in elections.

Furthermore, results from the 2011 and 2015 polls have revealed that Nigerians are much wiser than before and can prevent rigging if they want to. The fact that we are talking of the immaturity of our politicians means that we voted immature politicians into office. The electorate should be more circumspect in their choice of leaders knowing the enormous powers that will be bequeathed to them upon assumption of office.

Governors would be the Chief Security Officers of their states, both in words and in deeds, endowed with the capability to address any security challenge within their domain. The plethora of security challenges that bedevil our nation would be significantly reduced as the State Police would be dealing with a smaller terrain, using locals who will act as informants and spies to reveal the hideouts of criminals.

It will also solve the problem of under policing in Nigeria. According to information about the Nigerian Police gleaned from Wikipedia, there are about 371,000 policemen, 80% of whom are currently on VIP Protection Duties, leaving only 20% (about 76,000 policemen) to provide security for 180 million citizens. It will be a boon to the APC led federal government as most of the blame for the security challenges in the country would no longer be put on President Muhammadu Buhari but on the doorsteps of the state governors.

The roles and duties of the State Police should be clearly spelt out in the constitution. That should also include what would happen in the event of a clash between the Federal and State Police. It (State Police) would also create jobs for millions of teeming unemployed youths across the states of the federation. The use of militias, touts, thugs, and other criminally minded individuals to enforce state laws by governors, most of whom end up turning over to full blown criminality, would be a thing of the past with the creation of State Police. The issue of where to get the funds for State Police does not arise as most of the state commands of the current Federal Police are funded by the governors. All they need to do is to divert such funds towards the State Police.

February 15, 2018.

LESSONS FROM ZEXIT

South Africans received a perfect Valentine's Day gift from none other than Jacob Zuma, who resigned as State President in a nationwide broadcast. Dogged by corruption allegations, with over 700 corruption charges hanging over his head, and allegations of *"state capture"* owing to his inappropriate relationship with the wealthy Gupta family, Mr. Zuma is a cat with nine lives that ran out of lives.

After surviving half a dozen attempts to unseat him through a vote of no confidence in parliament, he was finally forced to resign by his own party apparatchiks who saw him as a national embarrassment and a dent on the party's image as they approach an election year. What lessons do we learn from Zuma's exit from power as a nation and as a people? Can Zexit - Zuma's exit - happen in Nigeria?

The first thing to learn is the concept of party supremacy in politics. Zuma was able to survive half a dozen opposition sponsored vote of no confidence in parliament, despite humongous corruption allegations against him, coupled with the fact that he was loathed by not a few, because his party, the African National Congress (ANC), stood solidly behind him. But the moment they withdrew their support, he knew that the game was up and he could not afford to swim against the tide.

This is in stark contrast to what obtains in Nigeria where party indiscipline is the order of the day. A case in point is the current leadership of the National Assembly which emerged against the ruling party's directives even though it had a majority in both houses of parliament. Closely related to this, is the absence of do or die politics -

apology to Chief Olusegun Obasanjo, the self-acclaimed proponent of do or die politics in Nigeria, - in South Africa. No political party in Nigeria can call on its members in power to resign from office as such calls would simply go unheeded.

As a matter of fact, it is extremely rare for a Nigerian politician to resign from office as they would rather destroy the party, state institutions and just about anything in a bid to hold on to power at all costs. Secondly, the presence of strong state institutions rather than strong individuals in South Africa, ensured that corruption allegations against Mr. Zuma was not swept under the carpet even though he was State President. Many of those corruption cases are currently ongoing and it is expected that Mr. Zuma would face trial in an open court since he no longer enjoys immunity from prosecution.

The wife of a Former President of Nigeria who had corruption cases with the EFCC, had them quashed after her husband's ascension to the highest office in the land.

Finally, the existence of a virile opposition and civic minded citizens who refused to be deterred until they saw the back of Jacob Zuma, is also another feature lacking in our democratic climate. Opposition in Nigeria thrives on mere rhetoric, all talk and no action, and the docility of the masses who bear the brunt of the bad policies of our leaders is stupefying.

February 20, 2018.

DECONSTRUCTING THE INSURGENCY WAR

The abduction of over a hundred school girls, by suspected members of the dreaded Boko Haram sect, at the Government Girls Technical Secondary School, Dapchi, Yobe State, was the most daring act in recent times, from a group that was proclaimed as *"technically defeated"* by the Buhari's administration.

During the administration of Former President Goodluck Jonathan, they staged several attacks both against public and private institutions, in several cities, even going as far as desecrating Abuja, Nigeria's capital city. They carted away several hostages including the famous Chibok girls, occupied territories (about 14 local government areas), and in an audacious move proclaimed a Caliphate in Gwoza, Borno State.

The militants gave the military a bloody nose. However, Buhari's election as President in 2015, changed the tide of the war. Boko Haram suffered one loss after another until Alhaji Lai Mohammed, Nigeria's Minister of Information, boldly declared on national television that the militants had been *"technically defeated"*. That "technical victory" is fast becoming a pyrrhic victory with the renewed wave of attacks by the insurgents on soft targets, and the recent abduction of over a hundred school girls.

Some have posited that the resurgence of the insurgents in recent times, can be attributed to the release of half of the Chibok girls, and the release of the abducted UNIMAID lecturers, where it is believed that large sums of money (several millions of dollars), and Boko Haram Commanders in Nigerian prisons, were exchanged for the freed captives. If this is true, that means the desire of the Buhari government to secure a political victory rather than a military victory over Boko Haram, possibly with an eye on the 2019 elections, coupled with pressure from the BBOG Campaign, pushed them into making a bad deal with the insurgents.

Boko Haram has killed 20,000 people and displaced 2.6 million people in a wave of attacks spanning a nine year period. Government should begin to think of long-term solutions to this menace rather than quick fixes because terrorism will not disappear from our midst overnight, as it is based on an ideology derived from a warped interpretation of religion, and there is no denying the fact that Nigerians are very gullible and susceptible when it comes to the issue of religion.

Nigeria's North East region (comprising 6 states) which is the epicenter of the insurgency is too large to be policed effectively by our security forces. With a landmass of 262,578 km, the North East is bigger than all the countries in West Africa with the exception of Ivory Coast. Members of the Armed Forces are not more than 250,000, all of whom are not stationed in the North East. Also, the Nigerian Police currently has 381,000 members, 80% of whom are on VIP Protection Duties. It is crystal clear that we do not have the requisite manpower to police the region and curb unfortunate incidents like the Dapchi abduction.

My solution to this shortage of security personnel is the creation of a National Guard and a Special Forces Unit in the Nigerian military. The National Guard (which some countries also refer to as the Republican Guard), will have chapters in all the states of the federation, will be federally controlled, and tasked with the responsibility of protecting the Nigerian State from external aggressors. They should be trained in counter-terrorism strategies and tactics, asymmetric warfare, and desert warfare.

Also, we should create a Special Forces Unit in the military that will be skilled in Search and Rescue Operations and endowed with the ability to launch precision strikes at enemy targets whenever the need arises. The issue of funding for these proposed security agencies does not arise as neighbouring countries with smaller populations and smaller economic resources already have these institutions operating in their security apparatus. That is the reason why Boko Haram has been unable to gain a foothold in those countries or cause any significant damage unlike in Nigeria.

In the interim, we should swallow our pride and engage international help in our efforts to decapitate the Haramists. American forces mentored the Iraqi forces that recently pushed ISIS out of Iraq. Why can't we explore such option in Nigeria?

A key issue which President Muhammadu Buhari must seriously look into is the issue of saboteurs within the military brass. BBC recently aired a report of how the Nigerian military was stopped from killing or capturing Sheikh Abubakar Shekau, the ruthless leader of Boko Haram, by a controversial order from *"above"* which delayed them for four days. Those within the ranks of the military who give controversial orders that impede efforts to crush the insurgency should be court-martialed and punished appropriately.

A military victory is what we should seek before a political victory. Boko Haram should be boxed into a corner where they will be forced to negotiate peace terms which should be devoid of exchange of cash.

February 27, 2018.

REINSTATEMENT OF NHIS BOSS

Last week's reinstatement of the suspended Executive Secretary of the National Health Insurance Scheme (NHIS), Professor Usman Yusuf, on the orders of President Muhammadu Buhari, has generated a lot of controversy. It would be recalled that Yusuf was suspended by the Minister of Health, Professor Isaac Adewole, in June 2017, following allegations of gross misconduct, nepotism, and theft of public funds to the tune of N919 million naira.

Labour, Civil Society Organizations and Opposition parties, have condemned the President's action, citing it as another example of the President's penchant for nepotism, favouritism and clannishness, and a dent on the government's anti-corruption war. Supporters of Yusuf and apologists of the government have on the other hand, claimed that most of the allegations against him are unsubstantiated, full of alterations, mix up in dates, and based on bias.

It is curious to note that Buhari ordered the reinstatement of Yusuf while none of the other 8 senior officers suspended along with him were recalled. Could this be because none of them is Hausa/Fulani? It is instructive to also note that one of the reasons why Yusuf was indicted by an administrative panel set up by the Minister was because of nepotism in appointments into the NHIS.

Yusuf allegedly recruited his kinsmen who were on grade level 10 in the State Public Service and imposed them on the staff of the NHIS by placing them on grade level 15 and above. Was his reinstatement a reward for recruiting kinsmen of the President into the NHIS and giving them appointments which they were unqualified for? Yusuf's arrogant statement that he could not report to the Minister since he was appointed by the President and not the Minister drips of nepotism. Would that statement have been uttered if the tables were reversed- A Southern Executive Secretary and a Northern Minister?

The consequences of Mr. President's action are too numerous to mention. Reinstating Professor Yusuf without recourse to the Minister who suspended him renders the Minister impotent and promotes insubordination both in the Health Ministry and in other Ministries headed by Southerners that have parastatals headed by the President's kinsmen. Investigations by the EFCC and other investigative bodies would be jeopardized as evidence would be tampered with, and potential witnesses will be threatened, sacked, redeployed or killed.

Another fall-out from this saga is that the NHIS boss is now independent of the control of the Minister and would be reporting directly to the President. The Minister would also be reluctant to act on issues involving NHIS and would rather stay aloof. More so, Yusuf would have no genuine respect for his boss, Adewole.

I am not surprised that Mallam Abba Kyari, Chief of Staff to the President, has been fingered as the brains behind this ignoble act. He is the head of the Presidential Cabal- according to Aisha Buhari, wife of the President - responsible for promoting tribal hegemony in the Buhari administration. I would not be surprised if Dr. Munir Gwazo, the suspended Director General of the Securities and Exchange Commission, who was suspended due to corruption allegations against him, is reinstated once he finds favour with Mallam Abba Kyari.

In other climes, Professor Adewole would have resigned his appointment but not so in Nigeria. Abroad, when people leave government, they go into high paying jobs in the private sector. In Nigeria, the reverse is the case because the public sector pays more than the private sector. I doubt if he would be able to resist the pressure from family, friends and well-wishers not to throw in the towel, because of the *"benefits"* that they derive from his occupation of such high office.

February 28, 2018.

ON THE ANTI-HATE SPEECH BILL

The anti-hate speech bill sponsored by Senator Sabi Abdullahi (Niger, APC), who is also the spokesperson of the upper legislative chamber, has attracted a barrage of criticisms. The bill seeks the establishment of an Independent National Commission for Hate Speeches to enforce hate speech laws across the country, and ensure the *"elimination"* of hate speech. It proposes some punitive measures for those who run foul of the law, but the part that has generated heated discussions among Nigerians, is where it proposes death by hanging for anyone found guilty for any form of hate speech that results in the death of another person.

For starters, the law is an over-kill. I stand to be corrected, but I do not think that there is any country in the world where hate speech is a capital crime punishable by death. Not even in rogue regimes, dictatorships, and illiberal democracies - apology to CNN's Fareed Zakaria - scattered around the world.

The million dollar question is *"How do we define hate speech"*? I am not talking about the dictionary definition but the metrics that will be used to determine what constitutes hate speech. Does hate speech uttered by a member of a tribe against his own people constitute an offence under the proposed law? I ask because in recent times two prominent Igbo politicians have used derogatory words to describe their own people. Does this constitute hate speech?

What about a scenario where a member of another tribe repeats exactly the same words used by these Igbo politicians, and it leads to a riot which results in loss of lives; can the *"repeater"* of the hate speech be prosecuted for committing a crime? Every literate Nigerian knows that there is a difference between criticism and hatred. But i doubt if our politicians understand that. In Nigerian politics, there are blurred lines between criticism and hatred, and both are viewed as one and the same. This has birthed fears among the populace that the proposed law is an attempt to gag dissenting voices. Governor Nasir El-Rufai of Kaduna State, recently pulled down the multi-million naira edifice belonging to the state chairman of a faction of the APC that opposes him. Beyond the gloat, triumphalism, and the threat to demolish another house belonging to a member of that faction, more worrying is what would happen to opponents of the governor when this bill eventually becomes law.

The fears expressed by many that this is an attempt to stifle free speech is definitely not out of place. Apart from politicians, many non-state actors like journalists, activists, political commentators e.t.c would run the risk of going to the gallows anytime they criticize any government policy or official. Subsequently, Nigeria would return to the dark days of military rule where we had freedom of speech but not freedom after speech - apology to Field Marshal Idi Amin Dada.

I am not a Lawyer but I know that there are enough laws in our statue books that pertain to hate speech. Prominent among them is the 2011 Anti-Terrorism Act which clearly spells out hate speech offences with the requisite punitive measures for violators devoid of capital punishment. Why are we attempting to reinvent the wheel instead of focusing on the implementation of existing laws? Or is there something sinister in the details of the bill which Nigerians are yet to discover? The creation of a commission for hate speech will increase the bureaucracy, increase our national wage bill, and create job for the *"boys"* which will make it open to bias as it will be infiltrated and controlled by the politicians, and used as a weapon of vendetta against their opponents.

Government should focus on healing the fault lines that divide our nation which is responsible for the rising wave of hate speech in the land. They should focus on the cause and not the actions alone. President Muhammadu Buhari should be just and fair to all the people of Nigeria irrespective of whether they voted for him or not, especially in the area of appointments into political offices. Another thing he should also focus on is how to ameliorate the biting poverty in the land. It is a truism that "a hungry man is an angry man". More true, is the fact that an angry man is liable to spew bile even when the occasion does not warrant it.

I am totally against hate speech most especially that which threatens the unity of the Nigerian state. But proposing a death sentence as punishment for offenders is akin to killing a housefly with a sledgehammer. Government should focus on what fuels hate speech and do the needful to stem this ugly trend in our society.

March 7, 2018.

IMO GUBER AND OKOROCHA'S ENDORSEMENT OF HIS SON-IN-LAW

2019 is just around the corner and political hopefuls are beginning to get endorsements from various groups and persons across the country. In Imo State, Governor Rochas Okorocha's overt and brazen endorsement of his current Chief of Staff and son-in-law, Mr. Ugwumba Uche Nwosu, to succeed him in Douglas House come 2019, has generated a lot of tension in the state.

Ordinarily, there is nothing legally wrong with a governor endorsing a candidate that he feels is eminently qualified to succeed him. But in the current circumstances, it is unethical as it drips of nepotism and the brazenness of it all stinks to high heavens. To put it in proper context, what Governor Okorocha is attempting to do is to install a stooge who is from the same senatorial zone with him (Orlu Zone), whereas the Owerri Zone where his deputy, Prince Eze Madumere, hails from has not produced a governor since 1999.

This betrays insensitivity to other zones in the state especially the Owerri Zone. And it is a gross violation of the state's zoning formula. Since his assumption of office as governor in 2011, Okorocha has ruled Imo state like his personal estate. Aside his nepotistic tendencies, reflected in the appointment of his son-in-law and sister into powerful positions in the state government, his many gaffes in terms of policies and utterances; the giving of state awards to supporters of his private foundation, using state funds to mould statues in their honour and organizing lavish banquets, all these are indicative of the inability of the governor to differentiate between the state and himself.

Like the French King Louis XIV who uttered those immortal words, *"L'etat C'est Moi"* meaning *"I am the state"*, Okorocha is Imo and Imo is Okorocha. The personalization of governance in Imo is an aberration to every known tenet of democracy. Part of the problem is that the governor is surrounded by yes men who lack the courage to say no to him or to any of his self-serving and anti-people policies. Another is the fact that the majority of the people in politics are in it because of the money hence would do nothing that would *"pour sand into their garri"*.

Meanwhile, Nwosu has also been endorsed by the state house of assembly and two local government areas in the state including his native Nkwerre local government area. It should be noted that in Nigeria's monetized politics, endorsement of candidates are often a function of cash changing hands. As a form of appeasement to his long-suffering deputy, Prince Madumere, who has been working for him in one capacity or the other since 1998, Okorocha offered him the Imo East senatorial ticket, even as he intends to vie for the Imo West senatorial ticket.

There are fears among the opposition that the machinery of state could be used to rig the gubernatorial elections in favour of Nwosu. Those fears may not be unfounded with the recent verbal assault on the Catholic Archbishop of Owerri Diocese, Dr. Anthony Valerie Obinna, by the governor's supporters, when the respected clergyman criticized the bad state of some roads in the state capital in his homily during a church service where Nwosu, and Okorocha's sister were present alongside their supporters.

It is a harbinger of what will happen to opponents of Nwosu as we approach 2019. Already, the rumour mill is agog with alleged plans to impeach Madumere, by Okorocha's kitchen cabinet, so as to provide a smooth sail for Nwosu's gubernatorial ambition. My thesis is that if Nwosu wins the APC ticket, the PDP or any other opposition party might benefit from protest votes within the ranks of the APC to produce the next occupant of Douglas House.

History might be repeating itself based on what happened in 2007, when against all odds, Chief Ikedi Ohakim emerged as governor due to the infighting within the ranks of the ruling PDP. On the flip side, due to the vagaries in politics, Okorocha might succeed in installing Nwosu as the next governor of the state. This means a continuation of Okorocha's anti-people policies and the state will be under the grip of one family for the next four years.

March 12, 2018.

MR PRESIDENT'S VISIT TO BENUE

Unlike what obtained in 2015, there were no mammoth crowds lining the streets to receive President Muhammadu Buhari as he visited Benue State this week to commiserate with the people and government over the loss of 73 lives in the New Year Day massacre by suspected herdsmen. Instead, the President met mammoth silence from a distraught people angry over his belated visit and his handling of the security challenge bedeviling the state.

What sent tongues wagging was the President's response to a complaint made by one of the Benue leaders, during an interactive session in the Government House. The complaint was that when the President told the Inspector General of Police, Mr. Ibrahim Idris, to relocate to Benue in order to get firsthand information about the Farmers/Herders crisis, he only visited and in less than 24hours departed for neighbouring Nasarawa State. He (PMB) replied saying he was unaware of the conduct of his appointee and explained that the meeting was not the right venue to expose the inefficiency of the police boss.

Femi Adesina, the President's spokesperson, is obviously a born again Christian. The only defence he had for his boss is that *"Mr. President is not omniscient"*. Meaning the President is not all-knowing. I find it strange that PMB is attempting a cover up for a subordinate who clearly flouted his instructions. In military parlance, Idris disobeyed a direct order from a superior officer, and nothing should stop him from facing the music. But I am cocksure that nothing will happen to him and this matter will eventually be swept under the carpet.

Appointments into public offices in Nigeria are usually based on the recommendation of godfathers and not on merit. Which means those appointed are loyal to their godfathers rather than their principal or the country. In the event that they run into trouble with their principal for an infraction of the law, the godfather steps in and no punitive measure is taken against the appointee. That pattern remains unchanged even after PMB assumed office in 2015. Does anyone remember the EFCC/DSS feud which resulted in the non-confirmation of Ibrahim Magu as EFCC Chairman by the Senate?

This revelation portrays the President as weak and not in control of the country. Also, his response highlights his bias and his insensitivity to the serial killings in Benue. Furthermore, it lends credence to conspiracy theories about the existence of a cabal in the Presidency. Come to think of it, If Idris can openly disobey his boss, then what stops junior officers under him (Idris) from also disobeying him? Definitely, we have a huge dysfunctional bureaucracy on our hands.

Mr. President missed a great opportunity to redeem himself in the eyes of the Benue people, through some of his actions during the visit. One, the banning of journalists from 23 media houses from covering the visit. Two, the cancellation of the proposed visit to the Tor Tiv and Chairman of the State Traditional Rulers Council, Professor James Ayatse. Finally, the cancellation of the proposed visit to the Internally Displaced Persons camp at Gbamjiba in Guma local government area. PDP's assertion that the President's visit was because of 2019 might be true after all. But one thing I know is that the APC will not win the Presidential election in Benue come 2019.

March 16, 2018.

SHEHU SANI AND SENATORS' SALARIES

When Sanusi Lamido Sanusi, former CBN governor-cum-Emir of Kano, told us some years back that a quarter of our annual budget was spent on the National Assembly, many did not believe him and tagged him a rabble rouser and an attention seeker. But the recent revelation about senators salaries and allowances by Senator Shehu Sani have proven Sanusi right. He revealed that a senator earns N13 million naira monthly for running costs which must receipted, N700,000 for personal salary and allowances and N200 million naira worth of constituency projects annually. However, the disclosure by the senator does not cover allowances for cars, housing, wardrobe, furniture, e.t.c which runs into several millions of naira. Unconfirmed reports a few years ago, indicated that our lawmakers budgeted N100,000 naira per head for their daily feeding allowance.

It is a tragic irony that while we have the largest concentration of poor people in the world, our lawmakers are arguably the highest paid in the world. Why can't they borrow a leaf from their counterparts in Britain, the House of Lords, where each lawmaker earns only 150 pounds (about N250,000) per sitting? How can we be paying corrupt politicians and thieving bureaucrats millions of naira as salaries and allowances in a country where no doctor, lawyer, engineer, university lecturer or any professional of any hue earns anything close to that amount monthly?

How can we expect to become a great power when for so many years till date, the Nigerian budget has been overwhelmingly tilted in favour of recurrent expenditure rather than capital expenditure? In most advanced climes, the private sector pays more than the public sector because remuneration is based on productivity and the public sector is seen as a place to serve and make an impact not as a channel to become rich. In Nigeria, the reverse is the case. Public service is a do-or-die thing because it is viewed by many as a cheap avenue to enrich self.

Judging based on productivity, I sincerely do not think that our lawmakers deserve to earn such humongous sums as salaries and allowances. Firstly, most of these senators do not have constituency offices. They do not hold town hall meetings and some rarely visit their home states. Secondly, the quality of debate in the senate is very poor and often characterized by absentee and sleeping senators during plenary. Thirdly, we have poor quality of senators. If it is not the dancing senator, or the singing senator, then it is the use of vulgar language on the floor of the senate or one malfeasance or the other. It is shameful that despite their lavish salaries, members of the senate are often accused of soliciting and collecting bribes to pass bills and from agencies that they oversee.

One knotty issue that baffles me and defies logic is the issue of constituency projects for lawmakers. Just like their name implies, lawmakers all over the world make laws, carry out oversight functions, and are vested with the power of appropriation while it is the role of the executive to implement projects. The earlier we do away with this democratic aberration, the better for our treasury.

I commend the courage of Senator Shehu Sani in making this disclosure unlike his counterpart, the Twitter Senator, who is adept at playing the ostrich and epitomizes the phrase *"all talk and no action"*. The way forward is to make lawmaking a part time job that pays allowances per sitting just as we had it in the First Republic. We should also do away with our current bi-camera legislature in favour of a unicameral legislature so as to save costs and reduce our recurrent expenditure.

March 16, 2018.

ABDUCTION OF DAPCHI SCHOOL GIRLS AND THE PREFERENCE FOR NEGOTIATION

The Federal Government of Nigeria prefers negotiation than the use of force to free 110 school girls abducted by suspected members of the Boko Haram sect some weeks ago. President Muhammadu Buhari made the disclosure during the visit of the former American Secretary of State, Rex Tillerson, to Nigeria last week. Unlike other terrorists acts globally, no group has claimed responsibility for the abduction several weeks after the unfortunate incident. Not to talk of setting preconditions for the release of the girls. So, who is FG going to be negotiating with for the release of the girls? If we believe the narrative of Aisha Wakil a.k.a Mama Boko Haram, that the girls are in the custody of Abu Musab Al-Barnawi faction of Boko Haram, then FG will have difficulty negotiating with him because his demands might be unreasonable.

Al-Barnawi is believed to be the first son of the slain founder of Boko Haram, Mohammed Yusuf. He could be motivated by revenge for his father's death and prove difficult at the negotiating table. We also run the risk of making abduction of soft targets by terrorist groups the norm, as it will be seen by the insurgents as a cheap way of making money to fund their operations. Is FG planning to go the same route that it did with the released Chibok girls which it exchanged for men and money thus providing oxygen for the already dying terrorist group to stage attacks in Dapchi and Rann? What exactly is going to be involved in this negotiation? Is FG going to pay a higher price than it did in the case of the released Chibok girls?

Garba Shehu, the President's spokesperson, said on a television programme monitored in Lagos that the Boko Haram commanders who were traded in exchange for the released Chibok girls were certified free of any threat to the Nigerian state by the security agencies before their release. Nothing could be further from the truth as recent evidence suggests otherwise. Shuaibu Moni, one of the freed commanders, went back to Sambisa Forest and recently released a video threatening to destroy Nigeria.

I am curious to know what manner of help Rex Tillerson, on behalf of the government and people of America, offered to the Nigerian government to enable it rescue the abducted school girls. Why did FG turn down the offer in favour of negotiation with the terrorists? A similar scenario played out during the abduction of the Chibok girls and those who are now in the government were the same set of people who criticized Former President Goodluck Jonathan for refusing foreign help. We need the Americans and any other foreign power willing to offer us help because our security agencies have proven over and over again that they have zero capacity when it comes to gathering intelligence to be used in fighting the insurgents.

We need their intelligence gadgets, and officers skilled in intelligence gathering techniques, data analysis, and search and rescue operations. It will not be out of place if the Nigerian security forces collaborate with foreign security forces to craft a whole new strategy to defeat Boko Haram and bring lasting peace to the North East. We should be proactive and not reactive in this war. It is highly unfortunate that the President attempted to score cheap political points by comparing his response to the Dapchi girls abduction to Jonathan's response to the Chibok girls abduction. That betrays insensitivity to the plight of the heart-broken parents of the abducted girls. A military victory is what we should seek before a political victory. I am not totally against negotiation but we should employ the carrot-and-stick approach on this issue. Box the insurgents into a corner and force them to negotiate from a position of weakness. That is the way forward.

March 20, 2018.

HOUSE RECALL OF HON. JIBRIN

Like a bird let out of a cage, Honourable Abdulmumin Jibrin, experienced *"freedom"* when the suspension placed on him by his colleagues for 180 legislative days in 2016, was lifted last week. The Kano lawmaker and former Chairman, House Committee on Appropriation, was suspended for exposing the padding of the 2016 budget by the leadership of the House. He had also accused the Speaker of the House of Representatives, Mr. Yakubu Dogara, of misappropriation and embezzlement of funds to the tune of hundreds of millions of naira.

Mention must also be made of the fact that the suspension lasted more than the stipulated 180 legislative days. However, he was not allowed to return to the green chamber at the expiration of his suspension because the leadership of the house demanded that he should write a letter formally apologizing for allegedly lying against them. He wrote the letter and although it wasn't fully read before the parliament, the speaker paraphrased it by saying he had apologized and met all the conditions given to him.

The silencing of Jibrin is a huge loss to the nation. Those who are trapped within the corrupt system will not have the courage to speak out and expose the shady dealings within the political class for fear of what will befall them. Events of this nature will act as a stimulus to a growing culture of conspiratorial silence in the face of tyranny and oppression of the Nigerian people. Now we know why the Twitter Senator, Mr. Ben Murray Bruce, lacks the spine to say the things he says on social media, on the floor of the senate.

In the usual Nigerian way, the allegations leveled against the speaker and the house leadership ceased to be investigated by the anti-graft agencies the moment the hammer fell on Jibrin, and the matter was quickly swept under the carpet.

Jibrin was prophetic in an interview he granted a Lagos-based television station at the inception of the budget padding scandal. He said failure by Mr. President and the anti-graft agencies to act on the allegations against Dogara and the House Leadership, would sound the death knell on the anti-corruption war. Not only did the anti-corruption war suffer a huge dent in terms of public perception, it is currently viewed as a selective witch-hunt of political opponents. Transparency International, the global anti-corruption watchdog, gave us a clearer picture when its latest rankings indicated that corruption was on the rise despite the anti-corruption war.

Buhari's handlers did him a great disservice by failing to encourage him to protect Jibrin, as he was on the same ideological page with the President on the anti-corruption war, despite several appeals from Jibrin and concerned Nigerians for him to do so. This failing contributed in no small measure in diminishing the President's anti-corruption war in the eyes of many Nigerians.

As a parting shot, I must state that PMB's war on corruption is at best selective. Though Former President Olusegun Obasanjo, was also accused of waging a selective war on corruption, he at least had the courage to prosecute members of his party, unlike what we have now where only members of the opposition party are prosecuted for corruption. Similarly, the ruling All Progressives Congress has become a house of refuge that anyone who has corruption cases to answer runs into and is free from prosecution. Can anyone in the administration explain what happened to the EFCC graft cases against Former Governor Orji Uzor Kalu, Former Governor Sullivan Chime, and Senator Musiliu Obanikoro, all former members of the PDP who are now in the APC?

March 20, 2018.

IGP'S ORDER TO WITHDRAW POLICEMEN FROM VIP'S

In an apparent move to secure his job and prevent a possible sack, following the brouhaha that trailed the revelation that he had flouted the President's order to him on the heels of the farmers/herders crisis in Benue; the Inspector General of Police, Mr. Ibrahim Idris, has ordered the immediate withdrawal of all police orderlies attached to private individuals and companies in the country. Exempted from this order are all private financial institutions across the country.

Mr. Idris, shot himself in the foot and sabotaged the effective implementation of his directive, when he gave state commissioners of police discretionary powers to determine who qualifies for police protection in their respective states. He also said he has submitted a memo to the President asking him to approve the categories of public officials who would be entitled to police orderlies. As soon as the President complies, the Police Chief would commence immediate implementation of the directive against public officials who have no presidential approval for police protection.

Going down memory lane, this order is not novel. Former Presidents Olusegun Obasanjo, Goodluck Jonathan, Late President Umar Musa Yar'adua, and even President Muhammadu Buhari have at various times given the police orders to withdraw their men from guarding VIP's. Also, Idris' predecessors in office, Ogbonnaya Onovo, Hafiz Ringim, Mohammed Abubakar, and Solomon Arase, have given such orders in times past and nothing came out of it.

Truth is, deploying policemen on VIP protection duties is a huge racket that yields billions of naira annually to the Nigerian Police. Most of these monies usually end up in the private pockets of senior officers in the force. An average MOPOL on guard duties gets N150,000 monthly. But that is not what the big man who enjoys the protection really pays.

The big man pays far more than that to the senior officer in the force usually a commissioner or an AIG, who takes out his own cut and gives N150,000 to the boys per head. There are currently 150,000 policemen on guard duties and if you do the math, you will discover that this is a cash cow for the Nigerian Police. Mike Okiro, Former Inspector General of Police and Chairman of the Police Service Commission, was euphemistic when he declared that the Police lacked the resources to withdraw personnel from private actors.

On the other hand, Senator Isa Misau, a former Policeman, was succinct when he accused the IGP of illegally pocketing billions of naira derived from posting policemen on guard duties to private individuals and private companies last year. He is currently undergoing prosecution by the police for blowing the whistle.

Our policemen who are constitutionally entrusted with the task of maintaining law and order in the society have been reduced to errand boys by VIP'S just because of their desire to make ends meet. It is not unusual these days to see policemen carrying the handbags of wives and girlfriends of these VIP'S. Some are sent to the market to buy foodstuffs, others are guarding filling stations, the children of the big men, or foreigners who do not enjoy such privilege in their home countries.

I do not begrudge VIP'S for seeking police protection. It is the norm all over the world for those who are successful to seek for some form of protection against fiendish elements in the society. The Nigerian situation does not help matters as only government security agencies are licensed to bear arms. How effective can a private bodyguard be without arms? At best, he is a toothless bulldog who can only bark but not bite.

The solution is to grant private security firms the right to bear arms so they can provide protection for private citizens who desire it, thus freeing up policemen to perform their statutory duties. Government should also look closely into the issue of providing police protection for government officials. Last year, we were informed by the police that over 200 policemen are currently attached to the Governor of Rivers State, Chief Nyesom Wike.

Multiply that figure by 36, including those attached to their deputies, commissioners, special advisers, judges, legislators (both state and federal), ministers, then we are talking of tens of thousands of policemen guarding people whose failed policies are responsible for the rising wave of insecurity in the land that they are trying to protect themselves from. It is my firm belief that if the Nigerian Security and Civil Defence Corps (NSCDC) is assigned the task of protecting government officials nationwide, it would perform creditably well.

My bet is that nothing would come out of this order by the IGP. If the IGP can openly disobey his boss, the President, what makes him think his subordinates would not act in a similar fashion towards him?

March 21, 2018.

IS BUHARI REALLY CORRUPT?

I will begin this piece definition of the word corruption. One definition of corruption in the Merriam Webster Dictionary is striking. It defines corruption as a dishonest or illegal behaviour, especially by powerful people such as government officials or police officers. Going by that definition, all politicians, nay mortals are corrupt. There are no saints on the earth. The saints triumphant are all in Heaven. I believe that when Nigerians talk about corruption that what they are actually referring to is financial corruption. And that is the province of this discourse. Simply, the contextual definition of corruption is the use of state funds or resources to enrich self.

The public perception that every Nigerian politician is corrupt is a myth that has no basis. For starters, there is a difference between personal corruption and government corruption. It is possible to be an island of probity surrounded by a sea of corruption. Major Chukwuma Kaduna Nzeogwu, who led Nigeria's first military coup in 1966, accused the Balewa government of corruption and killed the Prime Minister, only for us to discover at his death that the Prime Minister had only 10 pounds in his bank account and owned a mud house.

Chief Obafemi Awolowo was accused of corruption by his traducers, and was indicted by the Justice Coker Inquiry. Only for those responsible for his travails to confess many years later that he was innocent of all the allegations against him and asked for his forgiveness. I believe very strongly that we still have politicians in government today, who are not personally corrupt.

However, it must be stated that the dynamics of the world in which we live in, has made it virtually impossible for one to occupy a public office, serve meritoriously without stealing public funds, and still retire into poverty as it used to be in times past. Former American President, Bill Clinton, left the White House without owning a house. He moved into his wife's house in New York while his friends and supporters contributed money to buy him a house of his own. Today, he rakes in millions of dollars annually from paid speeches delivered in conferences and events around the world.

That brings me to the subject of the definition of money in today's world. Money is not limited to cash alone. Influence is money. Goodwill is money. A good name is money. Fame is money. Talent is money. Even beauty is money. And there are many more definitions of money. Money is anything that can be easily converted to cash. In today's world, it is extremely easy for a politician to convert any of the listed qualities into cash.

There is no law in Nigeria that states explicitly that a politician must be poor while holding public office. Poverty is not a sign of righteousness or incorruptibility. Politicians like the rest of us, have a right to aspire to the good things of life. We must also not mistake the perks and privileges of office as personal property. That some state governments in Nigeria own private jets does not mean that it is the personal property of the governor.

Rotimi Amaechi, Minister of Transportation, declared some time ago, that the Buhari government is corrupt but not as corrupt as the Jonathan government. I partially concur with his assertion. The Buhari government is corrupt. Babachir Lawal Saga, Mainagate, and $25 billion dollars NNPC contracts allegedly awarded without due process are a few instances of this administration's romance with corruption. What I do not agree with is the claim that the Buhari administration is less corrupt than the Jonathan administration. The full extent of the corruption in the Buhari administration cannot be known until their tenure in government lapses. Time will tell if Amaechi's assertion is totally correct or not.

Now to the meat of this discourse. Is President Muhammadu Buhari personally corrupt? The easiest way to identify a corrupt public official is anyone who lives above his means. Former Military President, General Ibrahim Badamasi Babangida, lives in a 50-room hilltop mansion, owns a private jet, several mansions within and outside Nigeria, several multi-billion naira enterprises through fronts, his children live like Arabian Princes, and an international magazine once listed him as the 85th richest man in the world in the late 80's.

However, if you calculate all his salaries and allowances as a military General and as Head of State for one hundred years, it is not enough to enable him afford such a fabulous and fairy tale lifestyle. Similarly, after his release from Abacha's gulag in 1998, Chief Olusegun Obasanjo told the world that all he had in his bank account at home and abroad was only N20,000. As President of Nigeria, he established a private university, expanded his farm to Cross River State, became a major shareholder in Transcorp, a company he set up and gave significant government patronage, built a multi-billion naira Presidential Library and hilltop mansion, bought banks, hotels, several landed properties in Lagos e.t.c.

Aside the impropriety of setting up business ventures as a sitting President, his total salaries and allowances cannot be said to be the source of his great wealth. Conversely, President Muhammadu Buhari lived a Spartan lifestyle devoid of opulence or luxury before his election in 2015 and no multi-billion naira businesses or investments have been linked to him since he assumed power till date.

He also declared his assets publicly which means Nigerians can easily know if he has corruptly enriched himself during his tenure in power. An act, previous Presidents did not do with the exception of Late President Umar Musa Yar'adua. Let me also add for the records, that I personally believe that Former President Goodluck Jonathan is not personally corrupt for similar reasons. Despite Buhari's predilection towards asceticism, and disavowal of conspicuous consumption, the lifestyle of his wife and children are diametrically opposed to his.

This can be explained. His wife hails from the super wealthy royal family of Adamawa state whose kingdom stretches to Cameroun and

Chad. Also, two of his female children are married to prominent billionaires in Nigeria. Furthermore, they have benefited immensely from the goodwill and the cult followership that Buhari enjoys in Northern Nigeria, among the talakawas and the bourgeoisie.

The allegation that Buhari was complicit in the $2.5 billion dollars missing oil money scandal in 1979, is unfounded and unsubstantiated. Former President Shehu Shagari set up the Justice Ayo Irikefe probe panel in 1980, to investigate the allegation of the missing money in the NNPC accounts during Buhari's tenure as Petroleum Minister. The verdict of the probe panel was that no funds were missing as those who made the allegations were unable to substantiate their claims when called upon to do so.

Similarly, Former President Olusegun Obasanjo set up a probe panel to investigate corruption allegations in PTF during Buhari's chairmanship of the body and he was exonerated of any wrongdoing. The Owu Chief, has stated repeatedly in several fora that the PTF investigative probe panel report did not indict Buhari. Though the report of the probe panel was never made public, vintage Obasanjo famed for his vindictive nature, would not have hesitated to use the report against Buhari when he contested against him for the position of President in the 2003 elections, if the report had indicted him.

The fault lines in our nation, in the run up to the 2015 elections, which made many vote along ethnic, tribal, and religious lines, are yet to heal. Instead, it has deepened due to the president's proclivity towards nepotism, his aloofness towards critical issues in the polity, his style of governance, and some of his utterances either personally or through his spokespersons.

Unfortunately, many still interpret issues in the polity according to those fault lines. Which is why no matter how educated or enlightened you are, even when the facts stare at you coldly in the face, as long as you did not vote for Buhari in 2015, you can never see anything good in him or his government. Psychologists call it Cognitive Dissonance. The rejection of the facts of an issue based on an emotional standpoint.

In conclusion, empirical evidence suggests that President Muhammadu Buhari is not personally corrupt though his government is corrupt. It is a fallacy to assume that every politician in Nigeria is corrupt. Also, people react to issues in the news based on their personal bias, from the prism of the political camp they belong to, their religious affiliation, or the part of Nigeria that they come from.

March 30, 2018.

2019: THE ODDS FAVOUR BUHARI

Last week's declaration by President Muhammadu Buhari, that he would seek a second term in office came as a surprise to no one. Opposition and critics of the administration feigned shock and surprise by their utterances, as it is an open secret that no Nigerian President or leader has ever jettisoned the idea of running for a second term in office, at the expiration of his initial term.

Buhari came to power in 2015 with so much goodwill and promise. Three years down the line, his actions, inaction, utterances, and style of governance have frittered away a lot of that goodwill. Buhari's sins are numerous. Nepotism, lack of communication with the citizenry, lethargic response to critical issues in the polity, selective prosecution of the anti-graft war, rising wave of insecurity, and non-adherence to the rule of law e.g. in the cases of Sheikh El-Zakzakky, Colonel Sambo Dasuki (rtd), and Mazi Nnamdi Kanu. However, he does have a few pluses.

One, he succeeded in lifting Nigeria out of economic recession which began under the previous administration in 2014, though biting poverty is still ubiquitous and endemic among the populace. His release of two bail-out funds and Paris Club Refunds (totaling over a trillion naira) to states is commendable as it was pivotal in lifting the economy out of recession.

Two, no matter what people think or say, his selective prosecution of the anti-graft war has only affected the guilty and not the innocents.

Those among the guilty who are currently being shielded from prosecution by the powers that be, will have their day in court someday when a Pharaoh arises that does not know Joseph.

PMB is going into 2019 with a lot of baggage unlike in 2015. One, the incessant killings by herdsmen coupled with his lackadaisical attitude and lackluster response to the issue, has eroded a lot of support for him, especially among those who have borne the brunt of these attacks. It has also fuelled conspiracy theories of the Hausa/Fulani agenda to take over Nigeria and rule as overlords over the rest of the country.

Two, the anti-graft war has negatively impacted a lot of looters who are major donors to Nigeria's influential Pastors and Churches. Recent revelations have shown that a lot of monies looted from our collective patrimony during the past administration, found its way into the churches.

For example, a major witness in the trial of Major General Emmanuel Atewe (rtd), one of the Army Generals accused of looting billions of naira meant for the purchase of arms to fight the Boko Haram insurgency during the past administration, confessed in an open court that the General instructed him to pay the sum of N35 million naira into a bank account belonging to Winners Chapel, one of Nigeria's numerous prosperity-gospel churches.

It must be said that most of these looters were the ones responsible for the anti-Buhari sentiments held by most Christians pre-2015, using the agency of the church through the Pastors. The stoppage of the free flow of corrupt money into the church as a result of the anti-graft war has resulted in the deliberate poisoning of the minds of a lot of Christians by their Pastors that the President is anti-Christian and has an Islamic agenda. Based on this, a lot of Christians are prejudiced and may likely not vote for the President come 2019.

Three, some of Buhari's actions, inaction, statements, appointments, and non-adherence to the rule of law, has deepened our national fault lines and made him lose a lot of support among Nigerians, many of whom now view him as a sectional leader with a natural predisposition towards clannishness. But all these challenges will not stop Buhari from victory in 2019. Certain factors will work in the President's favour.

Like his American counterpart, President Donald Trump, no matter what the Buhari does or says, it has no effect on his political base in the North. PMB still has a cult following and rock star popularity in the North. This fact was recently attested to by none other than Bishop Matthew Hassan Kukah, a man reputed for speaking truth to power regardless of whose ox is gored. Indeed, no politician in Nigeria today has the kind of following that he has in a region that is expected to deliver over 50% of the votes.

It is pertinent to state that in Nigeria elections are not won on social media or based on media popularity alone. Majority of those who criticize the President in the media, especially the youths, are either not registered to vote or would not come out to vote on election day.

Unlike what happened in the PDP pre-2015, there is no major rebellion or defection from the APC to any opposition party despite the chasm and friction within the party. The PDP itself has been hijacked by a cabal, and going by the recent utterances of some of those who lost out in the race for the National Chairmanship of the party last year, it contains a lot of disgruntled elements who would not hesitate to work against the interest of the party at the slightest opportunity.

Social Democratic Party (SDP), the acclaimed Third Force, which most disaffected politicians in the APC and the PDP have signaled their intention to decamp into, lacks a national spread, a formidable political structure, a calculated strategy, and political bigwigs who can enable them to wrest power from the ruling party, ten months to an election that they are hopeful of winning, unlike the APC which had all these and more about a year to the 2015 elections.

Fringe candidates like the Publisher of Sahara Reporters, Omoyele Sowore, Professor Kingsley Moughalu, former deputy governor of the Central Bank of Nigeria, stand no chance of winning the Presidential elections in 2019. They lack the money, the political structure, and do not possess the character defects that will enable them to make compromises in order to run on a larger political platform which would avail them of the money, the structure, and boost their prospects of winning significantly.

There are over 8,000 electoral wards in Nigeria and you need to have foot soldiers (party agents and supporters) in every ward for you to stand a realistic chance of winning the Presidency. Furthermore, PMB's rapprochement with the APC National Leader, Asiwaju Bola Ahmed Tinubu, would guarantee him bloc votes from the South West, with the possible exception of Ekiti, and also avail the APC Presidential Campaign of the political skills and strategies of one of Nigeria's most respected and most successful political juggernauts.

Most importantly, the voting demographics as released by INEC still favours Buhari. INEC voter registration as at January 2018 is as follows. North-Central = 10,586,965, North-East = 9,929,015, North-West = 18,505,984, South-East = 8,293,093, South-South = 11,101,093, South-West = 14,626,800.

From the figures, it is clear that there are more registered voters in the North (Buhari's stronghold) than in the South-South and South-East which is the stronghold of the opposition. Also, 90% of the political elite in the South West are in support of the President. So it is fair game to say that the President will carry the day in the region come 2019.

In conclusion, I am not God and my prediction of the outcome of the election is based on empirical data available to me, and the use of logic. However, barring the intervention of the divine, it is safe to conclude that Buhari will remain as President till 2023.

April 17, 2018.

RECENT REVELATION ABOUT MISSING CHIBOK GIRLS

Ahmad Sakilda, a freelance journalist and blogger with links to the dreaded Boko Haram sect, stirred a hornet's nest when he divulged on social media that only thirty out of the over a hundred abducted Chibok school girls in captivity are still alive. He went further to say that out of these thirty school girls that are alive, some have either become wives of Boko Haram commanders, or are suffering from the effects of Stockholm Syndrome, having clearly expressed a desire not to return home.

This revelation which coincided with the fourth anniversary of the girls abduction, sparked national outrage and triggered a media firestorm in which social commentators debated the veracity of his claims and the government's response to it. A close scrutiny of the messenger reveals that he is a reputable journalist who has had stints with several reputable local and international media houses in times past, and was not found wanting in any way in the discharge of his duties. UAE based Sakilda who hails from Borno, has credible links to the sect and has been involved in efforts by the government in times past to secure the release of the girls. He has no record of giving false information to the public on the issue of Boko Haram. Except he was deliberately misled by elements in the group, his message seems credible. Some of the released Chibok girls confessed that many of their colleagues have died through bombs, gunfire or snake bites. An attestation of this claim is the fact that some of the released girls came back on crutches, while others had varying degrees of injuries on their bodies.

It is an impossibility that with the heavy bombardment of Sambisa Forest by our security forces most especially since the inception of the Muhammadu Buhari administration, that some of the abducted girls would not have been victims of collateral damage. Information gleaned from videos released by the sect, revealed that some of the girls have been indoctrinated by the Haramists and have now become militants themselves. This makes them legitimate targets of the Nigerian military in the insurgency war. It is a logical assumption that if Shekau still had over a hundred girls in his custody, he would not have hesitated to use them as a bargaining chip for the release of his captured lieutenants and money, or for some respite from heavy bombardments by the Nigerian military. Undoubtedly, the girls are not with the Mamman Nur faction of Boko Haram because they could have easily traded them for the release of their captured comrades and money, rather than kidnapping school girls in Dapchi, Yobe State.

The logistical challenge of taking care of over 200 girls, coupled with the ineptitude and nonchalance of the previous government towards securing their release, might have forced the sect into selling some of the girls into slavery. Remember, Shekau boasted in the video released in the aftermath of the abduction that he was going to sell the girls. Also, they could have been used as human shields during exchange of gunfire with the military. What the government needs to do is to ask Boko Haram to provide a proof-of-life of the remaining over a hundred school girls in order to refute the claims made by Sakilda. The lame response of the government on this issue would not suffice. In the event that the girls are truly dead, the government should not be economical with the truth but should say it the way it is. That way the parents of the missing girls can experience closure knowing that they will never see their children again this side of the world.

April 19, 2018.

SUSPENSION OF SENATOR AND INVASION OF SENATE BY ANGRY NIGERIANS

Wednesday, the 18th of April, 2018 would forever be remembered as a day of infamy in the annals of Nigeria's legislative and political history. It was a day when some angry Nigerians, arguably constituents of suspended Senator Ovie Omo-Agege, stormed the red chamber of the National Assembly complex and made away with the mace. The mace is the symbol of authority in the legislature and any decision taken in the absence of the mace is deemed null and void in the eyes of the law.

This unfortunate and sad incident happened at exactly the same time Senator Ovie Omo-Agege *"forced"* himself into the senate chamber in violation of the ninety day suspension slammed on him by the senate the week before. However, Senator Omo-Agege has denied any link to the theft of the mace and the Police announced its recovery the next day. Investigations by the Police and other bodies are currently ongoing.

Undoubtedly, there is a nexus between the suspension of the senator, his "forced" entry into the senate chamber, and the invasion of the senate by some angry Nigerians. But not in the way that most Nigerians think. Senator Omo-Agege's sin which incurred the wrath of his colleagues, was that he in the company of nine other senators addressed a press conference in which he voiced fears that the reorder election sequence bill was targeted at President Muhammadu Buhari. That bill has been placed on suspension in the aftermath of the drama that took place last week.

According to the senate, that statement by one of their own within the precincts of the National Assembly complex, is an incitement of Nigerians most especially Buhari die-hards in Northern Nigeria against the senate. But our distinguished senators did not consider the revelation of the humongous salaries and allowances that they earn by Senator Shehu Sani, as an incitement of Nigerians against the senate despite the backlash that greeted it from all and sundry. They also did not consider it proper to suspend Senator Dino Melaye, a vocal acolyte of the Senate President, Dr. Bukola Saraki, for using obscene words to verbally assault Senator Oluremi Tinubu on the floor of the senate. They applauded Senator Eyinnaya Abaribe when he declared that the President is incompetent.

Speaking on the suspension of the senator, Mr. Kurtis Adigba, a public affairs analyst and one of Nigeria's brilliant legal minds, opined that *"Senator Ovie Omo-Agege was suspended in spite of a valid court order against suspending him. It is not in the place of the senate leadership to decide which court order to obey or disobey. The senate cannot be laying claim to the law and at the same time be in breach of the law. An order of court, no matter how unjust on the face of it, must be obeyed until it is set aside or revoked. The senate could have challenged the jurisdiction of the court to hear the matter, or make the order, but did nothing. Omo-Agege, was right in attending the plenary of the senate yesterday. And he should continue in the coming days"*.

The crux of the matter is that we have a senate that has constituted itself into an opposition party and a cog in the wheel of progress of the Buhari administration. Their pastimes includes flexing muscles with the executive and it's agencies, proposing unpopular legislation and passing resolutions that is not within their brief. A few examples to buttress my assertion are the face-off with the Customs boss, Colonel Hameed Ali (rtd), the anti-social media bill, the anti-NGO bill and the recent resolution calling on President Buhari to sack all the service chiefs. Regrettably, the senate cannot stomach dissenting views.

There is no legislative precedent in the annals of this country where a senator will be suspended for expressing a dissenting opinion or alternative view not held by majority of the members. How can an institution which is supposed to provide a forum for robust debate of the policies and programmes of the government, transmute into one that stifles free speech, and suppresses opinions and dissenting views of its members? Mr. Adigba, throws more light on this issue. Speaking ex-cathedral *"The senate is an important democratic institution where senators should be free to express their views and not be afraid of being suspended by an intolerant leadership. Democracy, is essentially about the freedom to hold and express views freely. The senate is not a military boot camp where the wishes of the commanders must be obeyed."*

I condemn the desecration of the hallowed upper chamber by some angry Nigerians. People should learn to stomach their angst and express their grievances through recognized legal channels. However, I see nothing wrong with Senator Omo-Agege's action since there was a valid court order against his suspension by the senate. The laws of the Federal Republic of Nigeria takes precedence over the Senate Rules which his colleagues relied upon to suspend him.

My grouse is that an entire oil producing region, made up of five million people, have been denied representation at the senate due to legislative dictatorship. In the event that there is an oil spill, or a natural disaster which claims the lives of thousands, or the need to cite one or two federal projects in the region, the entire Urhobo Nation who have contributed immeasurable human, material, natural, and financial resources to the Nigerian state since independence in 1960 till date, have nobody to speak for them or fight for them as occasion demands. This is a great injustice meted against my people. A note of warning should be sounded to the senate leadership that if this suspension is not reversed, it has the capability of heating up the polity and leading to a new wave of attacks on oil installations in the creeks of the delta by aggrieved militants.

April 21, 2018.

DINO THE DRAMA KING

When news broke earlier this week that maverick Senator, Dino Melaye jumped out of a moving police vehicle after his arrest by operatives of SARS, I was unperturbed and unfazed. Dino is the king of drama in Nigerian politics. It is not unusual to find a streak of absurdity in most Nigerian politicians. But Dino is different. He is the master when it comes to playing in the theatre of the absurd. Blessed by the creator with infinite capacity for drama, unusual eccentricities and proclivities, he is also endowed with the gift of gab and courage which some of his detractors have derisively referred to as Dutch courage.

His recent arrest by the Police is based on a slew of criminal allegations against him including murder, armed robbery, and illegal possession of firearms. These offences were allegedly committed in his native Kogi, where the Police were repatriating him to for prosecution before he transmuted into an actor, alleging that the Police in connivance with the state governor were planning to assassinate him once he sets his foot on home soil. Ironically, Dino and Governor Yahaya Bello were once pals.

He once declared at an event during the early days of the Yahaya Bello administration that the people of Kogi chose late Prince Abubakar Audu but God chose Yahaya Bello to be Governor. His arrest also coincides with the beginning of the recall process from the National Assembly by his constituents. Dino has alleged on several occasions that the recall process is orchestrated by Governor Bello and sponsored with the princely sum of N1billion naira.

Pundits have speculated that his arrest is a ploy by the powers that be to distract him so that he does not interfere in the recall process. That may be true. But what I find difficult to understand is why he employed all manner of tricks in the book to evade arrest by the

Police? Even if the charges against him are trumped up, he is not the first Nigerian politician to suffer such fate, just as he is expected to have known the risks of his profession before entering into it.

His idol, Dr. Bukola Saraki, also went through a similar ordeal recently and he embraced it stoically like a gentleman. Furthermore, according to Nigerian law, they can't hold him for more than forty-eight hours after which he will be charged to court and his lawyer will apply for bail on his behalf. So, what is the fuss about? People like Dino, famed for his flamboyant lifestyle and love of the good life are usually afraid of losing their freedom because they will be denied access to the pleasures that they enjoy.

As a student of the University of Port Harcourt, I was among those who hosted the Honourable Dino Melaye at an event on campus in 2010, after he was suspended for fighting by his colleagues in the House of Representatives. We were under the impression that he was fighting for the masses of the Nigerian people. His actions and antics in the eight Senate have proven that we were deluded in believing that he was a genuine radical fighting for the welfare of our people.

As a Senator, he is a prominent member of the cabal responsible for the anti-executive and anti-masses posture of the Senate. He has also courted several controversies. If he is not singing songs to spite his enemies, dreaming dreams, or mouthing obscene epithets against a female senator, then he is displaying pictures of his luxury cars on social media, hosting costume parties, or enmeshed in a certificate scandal. Dino is a stormy petrel that eats, breathes, and lives controversies. Though currently in the National Hospital recuperating from injuries sustained from his James Bond moves, the last may not have been heard from Dino. Nigerians should expect more drama from the drama king in the days ahead.

April 28, 2018.

THE END!!!

MUSINGS ON ISSUES IN THE NEWS